J. D. Salinger, Revisited

Twayne's United States Authors Series

TUSAS 542

Warren French reading *The Catcher in the Rye* for the umpteenth time on "some crazy cliff," Gower Peninsula, Wales, Summer 1987. Photograph by Michael Cox Dugan.

J. D. Salinger, Revisited

By Warren French

University of Wales, Swansea

TWAYNE PUBLISHERS

NEW YORK

J.D. Salinger, Revisited
Warren French

Copyright © 1988 by G. K. Hall & Company
All Rights Reserved
Published by Twayne Publishers

1633 Broadway
New York, NY 10019

Copyediting supervised by Barbara Sutton
Book production by Gabrielle B. McDonald
Book design by Barbara Anderson

Typeset in 11 pt. Garamond
by Compset, Inc., Beverly, Massachusetts

Printed on permanent/durable acid-free paper
and bound in the United States of America

printing number

10 9

Library of Congress Cataloging-in-Publication Data

French, Warren G., 1922–
    J. D. Salinger, revisited / by Warren French
        p.   cm.—(Twayne's United States authors series : TUSAS 542)
    Bibliography: p.
    Includes index.
    ISBN 0-8057-7522-6 (alk. paper)
    1. Salinger, J. D. (Jerome David), 1919–   —Criticism and
interpretation.   I. Title. II. Series.
PS3537.A426Z614   1988
813'.54—dc19   88-4851
                                                                                   CIP

for Micha,
who shared the last summer at Cornish Flat

Contents

About the Author

Warren French retired from Indiana University in 1986 and is now an honorary professor associated with the Board of American Studies at the University of Wales. He spends half the year in Swansea, enjoying the beauties of the Gower Peninsula, and then in the winter heads for someplace warm (New Orleans, Catalonia), paying periodic visits to Ohio University (Athens), which honored him with a Doctor of Humane Letters degree in 1985. Born in Philadelphia in the great literary year of 1922, he received his B.A. from the University of Pennsylvania and his graduate degrees from the University of Texas–Austin. During a forty-year career, he taught at Stetson University and at the state universities in Mississippi, Kentucky, Florida, Kansas, Missouri (Kansas City), and Indiana (Indianapolis), with visits to Appalachian State University, the University of Wisconsin–Madison, State College of New York at New Paltz, Dalhousie University, and Ohio University.

French contributed the first book-length critique of J. D. Salinger to this series in 1963, following books on John Steinbeck (1961, revised 1975) and Frank Norris (1962). He has also published *The Social Novel at the End of an Era* (1966) and edited a series of "decades" books on American fiction, poetry, and drama of *The Twenties* (1975), *The Thirties* (1967), *The Forties* (1969), and *The Fifties* (1971), as well as *The South in Film* (1981).

In 1974 French bought a summer home in the New Hampshire village of Cornish Flat, about two and a half miles downhill from Salinger's retreat, where he lived until 1982, enjoying the traditions of the state where his grandfather and several previous generations of ancestors had been born. In 1975, when Twayne Publishers moved from New York to Boston, French rejoined the fold as field editor for the contemporary titles in this series and also created and edited the Twayne Filmmakers Series of more than fifty volumes published between 1977 and 1987. In 1986, he contributed a long-overdue study of Jack Kerouac and the Duluoz Legend to this series, and he is currently at work on a companion volume on the less-celebrated contributors to the San Francisco Literary Renaissance.

Preface

The irony of the title of this book is that nobody visits J. D. Salinger at all without a rarely extended invitation, and certainly the least likely recipient of one would be a professional literary critic. Like many authors, Salinger feels that what he has to say can be found in his books and that readers need no outside guidance, although the tragic behavior of Mark David Chapman (John Lennon's assassin) might suggest otherwise. (Chapman inaccurately cited *Catcher in the Rye* at his sentencing to justify his actions [see Chapter Three, n.13].) Anyway, I bring no news about Salinger himself, as I will be revisiting only the writings he has with increasing reluctance committed to print.

The publication of this book has been timed to mark the twenty-fifth anniversaries of the publication of both my original look at Salinger's fiction and the last of Salinger's four authorized books. Since then he has published—and that many years ago—only a single story and granted only a very few generally uninformative interviews. Many have wondered how his reputation could survive such a long self-imposed silence, and it is this question that this book will essentially address. While thousands of works of fiction have appeared and disappeared since Salinger's one novel and three collections of thirteen stories were published over the course of a dozen years, his works have remained steadily in print in many languages throughout the world. *The Catcher in the Rye* has been selected by advisors to the U.S. Information Service as one of the twelve post–World War II American novels most likely to last, and it is one of only two novels among the seven influential "documents" selected in 1977 by *American Quarterly* (official organ of the American Studies Association) for reassessment.[1]

Periodically over the last quarter century new novels have been touted as the successor to *The Catcher in the Rye*. Some, like John Knowles's *A Separate Peace*, have firmly established a less conspicuous place for themselves among American novels of adolescence, but most, like James Kirkwood's *Good Times, Bad Times*, have dropped out of sight after a season of ballyhoo. How can the troubled voice of one distraught narrator have spoken for American youth for so long in so many languages?

I undertook the first edition of this book when Salinger's fiction had obtained hotly debated cult status with young American readers of the "silent generation." Even this one source of solace for the young was under heavy attack by respectable elders, and I explained in the preface that I intended my book "as a guide for those who, bedeviled by the inscrutability of the younger generation, are not simply content to throw up their hands in despair but wish to understand." By the time the book was updated for the U.S. bicentennial in 1976, enthusiasm for Salinger had somewhat waned after a decade of youthful activism. I wrote then that I hoped this edition might "introduce a younger generation to what their parents of the 'silent generation' of the 1950s read with enthusiasm because they thought Salinger voiced their views of the 'phony' world." I did not believe that the time had come to "relegate Salinger to the museum," nor had it. As the country has grown more conservative and the younger generation become increasingly vocation oriented and security minded, another restless counterculture is turning back to the writings of a man who has made a success of refusing to conform.

This book is not, however, simply another updating of an aging text; rather it is the product of a fresh start, made upon my retirement from forty years of teaching in American colleges and the completion of a book about another alienated writer—Jack Kerouac, who handled comparable problems of unwanted celebrity with much less success than Salinger did. I have reacquainted myself with all that Salinger has published to see how well it stands up a quarter of a century after I first read through his works in chronological order in one long sitting and to speculate why some of them have kept so well that they are still read with great relish by old admirers and new readers alike.

That earlier reading was undertaken in green, sunny Florida, where the story that first made Salinger a cult idol, "A Perfect Day for Bananafish," was appropriately set. Florida induces lethargy, and the strident tone of my early book reflects the effort of an ambitious young academic to break the spell of swamps and sea and use Salinger's creations to give form to his own discontent. This book was written in happy exile on the misty Welsh seaside only a few blocks from the family home of Dylan Thomas—truly one of the century's few nonexpendable poets—in a much more mellow mood, allowing me to view the tribulations of Holden Caulfield and the Glass siblings from the perspective of a Victorian suburb remote in both time and distance from the garish American scene.

Between these two exercises, I have spent much of a decade in the New England town of Cornish, New Hampshire, where Salinger has retreated, though to my knowledge I never even caught sight of him. All respectful persons learn in Cornish how much Salinger does insist on privacy and how much, in a usually nosey world, his wishes are respected by the residents of these remote hills, who cherish their own long-standing traditions of privacy. Perhaps the greatest irony of Salinger's career is that he has indeed found the "nice and peaceful" place that Holden Caulfield denies exists; but this is a happy irony in a world where expectations do indeed most often outrun fulfillments.

This book, like the writing of its subject's, has been very much a solitary labor. I am grateful to the classes of students who for twenty-five years have endured patiently my defenses of Holden Caulfield and his creator against the phonies who beset them. Roy S. Simmonds, who, though never a college professor, is the model of a scholar and a gentleman, has been most helpful in alerting me to such news as there has been about Salinger and supplying me with valuable British materials. Peter Freese, a German scholar who has a better sense of the United States and a more subtle command of its language than most of its residents, has broadened my vision by sharing his sense of Salinger's impact in Europe. The book is dedicated to a companion who has kept me in touch with a young point of view while sharing my old-fashioned one.

Warren French

Swansea, Wales

Chronology

1919   Jerome David Salinger born 1 January in New York City, second child and only son of Sol and Miriam Jillich Salinger.

1932   Enrolled in McBurney School, Manhattan.

1934   Enrolled in Valley Forge Military Academy, Pennsylvania.

1936   Graduates from Valley Forge Military Academy, after serving as literary editor of *Crossed Sabres,* the school yearbook.

1937   Visits Vienna and Poland with his father, reputedly to learn about ham and cheese importing business.

1938   Briefly attends Ursinus College, Collegetown, Pennsylvania, where he writes a column, "Skipped Diploma," which features movie reviews, for the college newspaper.

1939   Attends Whit Burnett's short-story writing class at Columbia University.

1940   First published short story, "The Young Folks," in Whit Burnett's *Story* magazine, paid twenty-five dollars; "Go See Eddie" in *University of Kansas City Review,* after rejection by *Esquire.*

1941   "The Hang of It" in *Collier's* (reprinted in *The Kit Book for Soldiers, Sailors and Marines*); "The Heart of a Broken Story" in *Esquire* sells first story about Holden Caulfield to the *New Yorker* in November, but publication delayed until 1946 by United States entry into World War II; classified 1-B by Selective Service and works on M.S. *Kungsholm* as entertainment director.

1942   "The Long Debut of Lois Taggett" in *Story;* "Personal Notes of an Infantryman" in *Collier's;* reclassified by Selective Service and drafted into U.S. Army; attends Officers, First Sergeants, and Instructors School of Signal Corps. Romantic correspondence with Oona O'Neill (playwright Eugene O'Neill's daughter and later Charlie Chaplin's wife).

1943   "The Varioni Brothers," first story in *Saturday Evening Post;* stationed in Nashville, Tennessee, with rank of Staff Sergeant; transferred to Army Counter-Intelligence Corps.

1944   "Last Day of the Last Furlough" and two other stories in *Saturday Evening Post*; "Once a Week Won't Kill You" in *Story*; sends Whit Burnett $250 as a contest prize for another young writer and proposes a collection of stories to be called "The Young Folks." After counter-intelligence training at Tiverton in Devonshire, England, lands on Utah Beach, Normandy, on D day and participates in five campaigns in Europe; meets Ernest Hemingway in September.

1945   Discharged from army. "Elaine" in *Story*; "A Boy in France" in *Saturday Evening Post*; "This Sandwich Has No Mayonnaise" in *Esquire*; "The Stranger" and "I'm Crazy" (first published story to include material used in *The Catcher in the Rye*) in *Collier's*.

1946   "Slight Rebellion Off Madison," another forerunner of *Catcher* in the *New Yorker*; ninety-page novelette about Holden Caulfield, accepted for publication but withdrawn by Salinger.

1947   "A Young Girl in 1941 with No Waist at All" in *Mademoiselle*; "The Inverted Forest" in *Cosmopolitan*.

1948   Begins long exclusive association with the *New Yorker* with "A Perfect Day for Bananafish," first story about Seymour Glass (31 January); "Uncle Wiggily in Connecticut" and "Just before the War with the Eskimos" also in the *New Yorker*; "Blue Melody" in *Cosmopolitan*; "A Girl I Knew" in *Good Housekeeping* is selected for *Best American Short Stories of 1949*. Moves to Westport, Connecticut.

1949   "The Laughing Man" in the *New Yorker*; "Down at the Dinghy" in *Harper's*.

1950   "For Esmé—with Love and Squalor" in the *New Yorker* and *Prize Stories of 1950*. *My Foolish Heart*, film version of "Uncle Wiggily in Connecticut," the only motion picture based on a Salinger story, released by Samuel Goldwyn Studio on 21 January. Early in the 1950s Salinger begins studying Advaita Vedanta under Swami Nikhilananda at Sumitra Paniter Ramakrishna Vivekananda Center in New York City.

1951   *The Catcher in the Rye* published 16 July. "Pretty Mouth and Green My Eyes" in the *New Yorker*.

1952   "De Daumier-Smith's Blue Period" in *World Review* (London), Salinger's only known story to be first published abroad. Discomforted to be selected as one of three distinguished alumni of the year by the Valley Forge Military Academy.

1953   Moves to Cornish, New Hampshire. Meets Claire Douglas at Manchester, Vermont. "Teddy" in the *New Yorker*. *Nine Stories* published 6 April.

1955   Marries Claire Douglas, 17 February. "Franny" (29 January) and "Raise High the Roof Beam, Carpenters" (19 November) in the *New Yorker*. Daughter, Margaret Ann, born 10 December.

1957   4 May, "Zooey" in the *New Yorker*.

1959   6 June, "Seymour: An Introduction" in the *New Yorker*.

1960   Son, Matthew, born 13 February.

1961   *Franny and Zooey* published 14 September.

1963   *Raise High the Roof Beam, Carpenters and Seymour: An Introduction* published 28 January.

1965   "Hapworth 16, 1924" in the *New Yorker*.

1967   Divorce granted Claire Salinger at Newport, New Hampshire (Sullivan County seat), in November.

1974   *Complete Uncollected Short Stories of J. D. Salinger,* an unauthorized edition, published in two volumes, apparently in Berkeley, California, by still-unidentified persons; Salinger denounces violation of his privacy in his first public statement in years to Lacey Fosburgh, San Francisco correspondent for the *New York Times.*

1986   Suit against San Francisco booksellers over the pirated collection of short stories settled in Salinger's favor; Salinger granted an injunction against the publication of an unauthorized biography by British writer Ian Hamilton.

1987   Joins other *New Yorker* contributors in a protest in January against the replacement of editor William Shawn by new publishers. 8 March, Son Matthew (Matt) stars in the CBS telefilm *Deadly Deception.* Injunction against publication of Ian Hamilton's unauthorized biography made permanent in November when U.S. Supreme Court refuses to review the verdicts of two lower federal courts that upheld Salinger's objections.

1988   Kevin Sim's *The Man Who Shot John Lennon* telecast on British ITV, 2 February; Ian Hamilton's rewritten *In Search of J.D. Salinger* published (excerpts in May issue of *Vanity Fair*).

Chapter One
"That David Copperfield Kind of Crap"

Borrowed from my earlier book, this chapter title ultimately derives from Salinger himself, who used it in *The Catcher in the Rye* to describe the detestation he shares with Holden Caulfield of exposing Dickensian details about "his lousy childhood." Despite their aversion against curiosity seekers, even the historian disinclined toward rooting through wastebaskets feels obligated to summarize the public record.

Since Jerome David Salinger has for some years been a devoted student of Advaita Vendanta Hinduism, one way to approach the little we know about him is in terms of the Vedantic concept of the four *asramas* (stages) of life, as explained by one of Salinger's teachers, Swami Nikhilananda, who is quoted in Eberhard Alsen's *Salinger's Glass Stories as a Composite Novel*: "The full life period was divided into four stages, namely, brahmacharya, garhasthya, vanaprasthya, and sannyasa. The first stage was devoted to study. . . . The second stage was devoted to household duties [after the previously celibate young man took a wife]. . . . The third stage commenced when . . . the householder consigned the responsibility of the home to his children and retired with his wife into the forest [for meditation. . . . During the final stage], having renounced the world, he became . . . a wandering monk, . . . honored as a spiritual leader of society."[1]

Whether Salinger will ever emerge from the forest to enter upon such a fourth stage is beyond speculation, but his life thus far bears a noteworthy similarity to this ancient model, although the three somewhat uneven periods can best be characterized as those of acting (first in person and then through spokespersons), of creating a family both literally and metaphorically, and finally indeed withdrawing into the forest that is again covering New Hampshire hills after a period of despoliation.

Performer

The one thing that we know certainly about the young Jerry Salinger is that he aspired to be an actor. During the summer of 1930, when he was eleven, he was voted the most popular actor at Camp Wigwam, Harrison, Maine, a boys' boarding camp that must have been much like the one unpleasantly described in "Hapworth 16, 1924."[2] When in 1932, he entered the private McBurney School in Manhattan, he told the interviewer that he was primarily interested in dramatics, and he reportedly played principally female roles in school productions.[3] When he transferred in 1936 to Valley Forge Military Academy in Pennsylvania, he also became a member of Mask and Spur, the dramatic organization (though here he also joined the Glee Club, the Aviation Club, the French club, and the Non-Commissioned Officers' Club).[4] The high point of his theatrical career was apparently his position in 1941 as an entertainment director on the Swedish cruise ship M.S. *Kungsholm,* one of his few ventures that he has mentioned several times to interviewers.[5] He drew upon it for his short story "A Young Girl in 1941 with No Waist at All." In March 1940, just after his first short story was accepted for commercial publication, he wrote Whit Burnett that he wanted to write plays and act in them himself;[6] and as late as 1946 Hemingway's biographer, Carlos Baker, says that Salinger wrote Hemingway that he wanted to play Holden Caulfield himself in a play that he was writing.[7]

His interests began to turn to writing fiction, however, by the time he entered the Valley Forge Military Academy in 1936. While briefly enrolled at Ursinus College in 1938, he wrote a humorous column for the college newspaper; but he turned to more serious composition when he left college to return to New York City and enroll in Whit Burnett's well-reputed course in short-story writing at Columbia University. Burnett was also the editor of *Story,* which had a unique record for encouraging talented young people, having presented the first commercially published stories of Norman Mailer, Willian Saroyan, Tennessee Williams, and Truman Capote. Burnett was apparently the first and only teacher to make a profound impression on the wary Salinger, who later wrote a tribute to him that appeared posthumously in *Fiction Writers' Handbook* (1975), as Salinger's last known appearance in print.[8]

Although Burnett seems not at first to have paid much attention to the quiet young man, he was impressed enough with Salinger's first story, "The Young Folks," turned in near the end of the semester, to pay twenty-five dollars to publish it in *Story* in spring 1940.[9] Although some rejections followed, Burnett's move started Salinger steadily on a course that led to publication in the well-paying "slick" magazines of the time like *Collier's* and the *Saturday Evening Post* and even in 1941 to acceptance by the *New Yorker*, then as now regarded as the most prestigious and best-paying outlet for a young writer. America's entry into World War II prevented the publication of the story until 1946, when it appeared in revised form; but few other aspiring writers were to be buoyed through the war by the encouragement of such early recognition.[10]

Salinger had just celebrated his twenty-first birthday on New Year's Day, 1940, when Burnett's acceptance of "The Young Folks" launched his career. He was born on 1 January 1919 to Sol and Miriam (originally Marie) Jillich Salinger. His father remains as shadowy a patriarch as Holden Caulfield's or the Glass tribe's. He was born apparently in Cleveland, Ohio, possibly the son of a rabbi; but he had drifted far enough from orthodox Judaism to become an importer of European hams and to marry a gentile, Scotch-Irish Marie Jillich, who changed her first name to fit better into her husband's family.[11] They had one other child, a daughter Doris, eight years older than Jerry, who retired after working as a dress buyer at Bloomingdale's fashionable East Side Manhattan department store.[12] (Little is known about her, since she has steadfastly avoided interviewers.)

Information about Salinger's childhood is scanty, but Ian Hamilton, researching an unauthorized biography, discovered that the family moved several times during Jerry's early years to increasingly affluent neighborhoods. Beginning far uptown at 3682 Broadway, the Salingers moved in 1919 to 113th Street in Columbia University's Morningside Heights area. By 1928, they were down near Central Park at 221 West 82nd Street, and four years later during the depression they moved to Park Avenue at 91st Street, near the Metropolitan Museum of Art—a location that Vincent Caulfield mentions as Holden's family residence in "This Sandwich Has No Mayonnaise." Before entering the army during World War II, Salinger used 1133 Park Avenue as a return address.[13]

Salinger was apparently a mediocre student. The most detailed account of his scholarly performance, however, meticulously compiled out of his 201 file at Valley Forge Military Academy for the Philadelphia *Bulletin*, shows that Holden Caulfield was not sedulously modeled on his creator, who earned his only diploma creditably. His marks in

English varied from 75 to 92; and his final grades in June 1936 were: English 88, French 88, German 76, History 79, and Dramatics 88. His I.Q. is recorded in the file as 115.[14] (While such scores must be regarded with extreme caution, this one accords with others mentioned elsewhere and indicates that though of above average intelligence, Salinger was certainly not in the "genius" category in which he placed the Glass family siblings.) During his senior year at Valley Forge, he also served as literary editor of the class yearbook, *Crossed Sabres,* to which he contributed a three-stanza poetic tribute to the academy that has been set to music and was still being sung in 1971 at the last formation before graduation. He could have used his position also to write the class prophecy, which includes the prediction that he would write "four-act melodramas for the Boston Philharmonic Orchestra."

The two years after Salinger's graduation are poorly documented. William Maxwell, a fellow novelist and sympathetic admirer also associated with the *New Yorker,* wrote for the *Book-of-the-Month Club News* in 1951 using information apparently derived from Salinger: "In the midst of his college period, his father sent him to Europe for a year to learn German and to write ads for a firm that exported Polish hams. It was a happy year. He lived in Vienna, with an Austrian family, and learned some German and a good deal about people, if not about the exporting business. Eventually he got to Poland and for a brief while went out with a man at four o'clock in the morning and bought and sold pigs. . . . he hated it."[15]

These events must have occurred mostly during 1937, for it is unlikely that with some Jewish ancestry, Salinger would have felt comfortable in Austria after Hitler's *Anschluss* following his invasion on 11 March 1938. The information provides, however, a background for understanding his familiarity with the scenes described in "A Girl I Knew," one of his most affecting stories.

During the autumn of 1938 he was enrolled at Ursinus College, a coeducational liberal arts school sponsored by the Evangelical and Reformed Church (now merged into the United Church of Christ in America) at Collegeville, Pennsylvania, not far from Valley Forge. He remained only nine weeks, principally to write movie reviews for his column prophetically named "Skipped Diploma" in the college newspaper. He was soon back in New York, probably bored by a conservative rural school with a student body interested most in decorous socializing, intent on launching a career as a writer, beginning with Whit Burnett's nondegree course at Columbia.

Then just as Salinger seemed on the verge of a meteoric career, the Japanese strike at Pearl Harbor plunged the United States into World War II. Salinger may have been cruising the Caribbean on the M.S. *Kungsholm* on the fatal day, for the ship did not return from a trip like the one he describes in "A Young Girl in 1941 with No Waist at All" until 8 December, after which it was commandeered by the United States and converted into a troopship. (Salinger describes this transformation in the story, but in an early example of his characteristic finickiness, he does not set the story on the *Kungsholm*, but describes it as another ship, "anchored sleepy and rich, just a few hundred feet aft" in Havana harbor.)

Following the reinstatement of the military draft after President Roosevelt's declaration of a limited national emergency in September 1939, Salinger had been classified 1-B because of some minor heart condition; but in 1942, he was reclassified and drafted into the army and sent to a Signal Corps school. After being stationed in Nashville, Tennessee, with the rank of Staff Sergeant, he applied for Officers' Candidate School. He was transferred instead to the Army Counter-Intelligence Corps and shipped to England for training at Tiverton in Devonshire near Exeter (the probable venue for the first part of "For Esmé—with Love and Squalor"). He was landed on Utah Beach in Normandy with the U.S. Army Fourth Division on D day, 6 June 1944, and participated in five campaigns in the European theater as one of two special security agents for the Twelfth Infantry Regiment.[16] Although he abandoned hopes of producing a novel during this period of service, he made good use of the time to turn out a series of stories about GI's for "slick" magazines, as the respectable newsstand competitors with the Western and detective "pulps" were called.

Little more was heard of theatrical aspirations. A career in the performing arts would seem an unlikely one for a man with such dislike of publicity and personal appearances; but the final blow to any lingering fascination with the entertainment world surely came with the release in 1950 of Samuel Goldwyn's film *My Foolish Heart*, adapted by Julius and Philip Epstein (also responsible for *Casablanca* among many other screenplays) allegedly from Salinger's "Uncle Wiggily in Connecticut." Lawrence J. Epstein (no kin) in his tribute to Goldwyn's distinguished career as an independent filmmaker skips over this disaster, which tortures Salinger's fable contrasting the "nice" and "phony" worlds into a pictorial background for the sappy popular song that provides the title. Susan Hayward asks an old buddy she has betrayed the short story's climactic question, "I was a nice girl, wasn't I?" only ten minutes into the ninety-eight minute film. Salinger and the Epsteins had different senses of the word *nice*; Salinger had in mind the innocent, caring world of the Glass family—to Hollywood it meant *chaste*. His poignant tale of a loss of carefree innocence becomes a squalid tale of the loss of virginity. Salinger would never again sell film or television rights to any of his writings. The script has never been published, but one of the most curious pieces of Salingerana is a 128-page pamphlet, which contains a story in Danish, titled *Mit dumme hjerte*, which Victor Skaarup derived from the movie.

Puppeteer

Asked by Betty Eppes in 1980 why he published, Salinger replied that he had not foreseen what was going to happen, and he had certainly not wanted what did happen after the publication of *The Catcher in the Rye*. He was as obviously unprepared for the kind of cult success that he uniquely experienced in his generation as Jack Kerouac was several years later following the deferred publication of *On the Road* (which had been written the year *Catcher* was published). As I have commented in *Jack Kerouac*, Americans, especially those who grew up during the depression, were not trained for success, particularly in a risky field like fiction writing, so that the rare success a few enjoyed often proved more demoralizing than rewarding. Salinger could not even tell Eppes why he wrote, calling writing "a highly personal art." He said he did not really know if he had consciously opted for it or just drifted into it. [17]

Although he had quickly established himself in a position that most of his contemporaries would have envied as a writer for the "slicks," Salinger's work through the first decade showed no signs of attracting the attention his later stories did. It appeared that he might enjoy a comfortable future as a short story writer like *Saturday Evening Post* favorite Clarence Buddington Kelland or most glamorously, *New Yorker* staple John O'Hara—a position he probably could have handled as someone who had not become a face in the crowd.

There were two principal outlets for short story writers in the 1930s and 1940s—the prestigious but rather poor-paying quarterlies, like Alexander Cappon's *University of Kansas City Review*, where Salinger placed his second story, generally sponsored by prestigious schools, and the well-paying but disdainfully regarded "slicks" like *Esquire*, a market that practically disappeared with the demise of popular favorites like *Collier's* and *Liberty*. Only at the very top of the heap did Harold Ross's *New Yorker* make prestige profitable.

Salinger may have tried the route through the quarterlies, but only "Go See Eddie" has been located in one of the academic or private press journals. (Three more stories have been found in Whit Burnett's *Story*.) Apparently Salinger did not need to be nursed by these usually limited circulation journals, for beginning in 1941 he was reaching mass audiences with stories like "The Hang of It," an example of the then very popular short, short story, which could be printed in its entirety on one large page and read in a few minutes in the barber shop or beauty parlor. It appeared in *Collier's,* and a similar piece, "The Heart of a Broken Story," in *Esquire.* He even won the coveted prize of acceptance by the *New Yorker,* though publication was delayed by the war.

In 1942, another short, short, "Personal Notes of an Infantryman," appeared in *Collier's*. Salinger even sold a story called "Paula" to *Stag,* one of the men's magazines kept out of young people's reach, though this tale has never been published. His induction into the army probably slowed down his production, but in 1943 "The Varioni Brothers" appeared as his first contribution to the enormously popular five-cent weekly *Saturday Evening Post,* which published three more stories in 1944, including "Last Day of the Last Furlough," the first of a series about the hardships of soldiers separated from their loved ones; it included mention of the first version of Holden Caulfield as a young soldier missing in action. More stories about him and his bereaved brother Vincent (subsequently killed in action himself) and Vincent's teddy-bear-like pal Babe Gladwaller and his little sister turned up in 1945 in the *Post, Collier's,* and *Esquire,* even though the war was winding down.

A later Holden surfaced in print that year in "I'm Crazy" in *Collier's* and the next in the *New Yorker's* long-delayed "Slight Rebellion Off Madison." William Maxwell even later reported that Salinger had had a ninety-page novelette about Holden accepted for publication in 1946, but that he withdrew it to rewrite it. His appearances for the next year were limited to slick women's magazines, *Mademoiselle* and *Cosmopolitan,* which carried (and then reprinted in 1961 over the author's strenuous protests) "The Inverted Forest," his longest work with no character from either the Caulfield or Glass family; it presents a vision peculiar for Salinger of the long sufferings of the artist matched only by something like Tennessee Williams's play *Suddenly, Last Sum-*

mer. Salinger has never chosen to pursue this theme, and few of his fans are familiar with this atypical story.

His work did not appear again in the *New Yorker* until 31 January 1948, when he began an almost uninterrupted association with the sophisticated weekly. The story that began this association was, however, to change Salinger's life. "A Perfect Day for Bananafish" introduces Seymour Glass on the day of his suicide. No one could possibly have guessed then that this seriously disturbed army veteran would dominate Salinger's last published fictions or that Seymour's fictional suicide might become an event perhaps as much discussed as Mahatma Gandhi's assassination on 30 January. The cryptic tale quickly exercised, however, an obsessive fascination over neurotic young members of a generation that was to be stunned into silence by watching the brief euphoria following victory in World War II deteriorate into paranoia following the descent of an iron curtain in Europe and the rise of the McCarthyist witch hunters in the United States.

The story did not achieve its full impact, however, until the publication of *The Catcher of the Rye* on 16 July 1951 made Salinger's name a household word and whetted appetites for more of his fiction. In 1953, a collection of nine earlier stories he had chosen to preserve is led off by the Bananafish fable. In the interim between Seymour's periodical and hardcover appearances, Salinger had published "Blue Melody," based on the sad history of black blues singer Bessie Smith, in *Cosmopolitan,* and "A Girl I Knew," one of his tenderest tragic tales of the lost world before the holocaust, in *Good Housekeeping.* (It was selected for Martha Foley's *Best American Short Stories of 1949,* one of only three of his stories to be honored in such annual collections.) The only other story, "Down at the Dinghy," to appear in an American magazine outside the *New Yorker* introduced a second member of the Glass family, sister Boo Boo, in *Harper's* in April 1949. It was also included in *Nine Stories.*

From this point on, with the curious exception of "De Daumier-Smith's Blue Period," which is the only Salinger work known to have appeared first outside the United States and his only short story not to have appeared in an American periodical (it appeared in London's *World Review* in May 1952 before its inclusion in *Nine Stories*), Salinger was the *New Yorker's* man. "Uncle Wiggily in Connecticut" (20 March 1948), "Just before the War with the Eskimos" (5 June 1948), "The Laughing Man" (19 March 1949), "For Esmé—with Love and Squalor," perhaps still his best-loved story (8 April 1950). His darkest tale,

"Pretty Mouth and Green My Eyes" (14 July 1951), appeared in un-
paralleled (for Salinger) rapid succession. After the furor engendered
by the unexpected response to *Catcher,* there was a wait of almost
breathless anticipation for "Teddy," which turned up in the *New Yorker*
of 31 January 1953, scarcely two months prior to the publication of
the collection in April.

Early reviews did not suggest that *The Catcher in the Rye* would become the classic novel of its generation. Only the *New Yorker* understandably rolled out the red carpet with a five-page laudation by
regular contributor, playwright S. N. Behrman (11 August 1951). The
New York Times and the venerable *Herald Tribune* were evasive: Virgilia
Peterson dodged the issue in the *Tribune* (15 July 1951) with the opinion that Holden Caulfield's contemporaries would "constitute the real
test of Mr. Salinger's validity" (as indeed they have). The specifically
literary advisors—*Booklist, Library Journal, Saturday Review*—were impressed; but except for *Harper's,* the general magazines for the concerned and thoughtful—*Atlantic, Nation, New Republic*—were less so.
The *United States Quarterly Book Review* (sponsored by the Library of
Congress) and the *Catholic World* launched a flotilla of complaints
against the excessive use of teenage profanity. The dissident viewpoint
was summed up in *Commentary* by William Poster, an editor of *American Mercury,* who attacked both the novel and the *"New Yorker* school,"
complaining that *Catcher* could be distinguished from comic strips like
"Our Bill" and "Penny" (then features of the now defunct *Herald Tribune*) not "by superior depth but a different kind of selectivity and a
different set of conventions." The *New Yorker* school, he asserted, "has
run down because it cannot be recharged from the battery of some
viable, positive approach to culture, morals, religion, or politics."[18]

Catcher did not at first sell as well as *Franny and Zooey* subsequently
did. Although it made the best-seller list in the *New York Times Book
Review,* it never reached the top. *The Caine Mutiny, From Here to Eter-
nity,* and Nicholas Monsarrat's *Cruel Sea* monopolized the top three
positions during the ten weeks from 19 August to 21 October 1951
when *Catcher* reached the fourth spot, which was the peak of its popularity. It remained on the list for twenty-nine weeks, about as long
as *Franny and Zooey* held first place in 1961 at what was probably the
peak of Salinger's popularity. It last appeared in twelfth place on 2
March 1952, while Herman Wouk's *Caine Mutiny* returned to the top
and monopolized the year's awards for best novel.

Catcher was successful enough, however, to upset Salinger. He became disturbed by the enormous close-up of his face on the dust jacket. At his request, it was removed from the third and subsequent edition of the book. He was less successful in avoiding fans. Although he admitted to Eloise Perry Hazard that "many of the letters from readers have been very nice," he told her, "I feel tremendously relieved that the season for success for *The Catcher in the Rye* is nearly over. I enjoyed a small part of it, but most of it I found hectic and professionally and personally demoralizing."[19] She reported that to avoid publicity he had fled to Europe.

He returned to find, however, that the season for success had not ended. Valley Forge Military Academy selected him in 1952 as one of its three distinguished alumni of the year and asked him to attend a ceremony to receive an award. His sister, Doris, replied that he was in Mexico, but in June he wrote to thank the school for the award, which he said made him somewhat uneasy.[20] Not prepared to deal with the monster he had created inadvertently, he fled his bachelor home in fashionable Westport, Connecticut, for the New Hampshire hills. He published no new fiction for two years. He had become the prisoner of his own fabulous creations.

When in April 1956 Frederick Gwynn, as head of the newly appointed Emily Clark Balch Committee to select a writer-in-residence for the University of Virginia, wrote to Salinger about becoming the first appointee to the post that was subsequently accepted in 1957 by William Faulkner, Salinger disqualified himself. Faulkner's biographer, Joseph Blotner, reports it was "because he had done that kind of thing once and found it was not for him.[21] (Blotner was the co-author with Gwynn of the first important critique of Salinger's work.)

Householder

A new life did, however, begin for the isolated bachelor in 1955. After going upriver to Cornish, Salinger, despite the regard his characters express for *The Great Gatsby,* chose to disregard Nick Carraway's key warning to Fitzgerald's doomed romantic: "You can't repeat the past." Salinger became a pal of some local high school students (Bruce Bawer quotes one of them later remembering, "He was just like one of the gang").[22] This idyll lasted until two of them—one named Shirley Blaney—interviewed him for the weekly high school page of the Claremont (New Hampshire) *Daily Eagle.* This somewhat gushing account appeared, however, on the front page of the ill-fated Friday, 13 November, edition of the *Eagle* as a "scoop." Much has been made of the episode in earlier accounts as a seeming betrayal by kids grabbing for "the gold ring" that further alienated Salinger from society. In more recent versions of the incident, however, some of the former "gang" recall no sudden break with Salinger, but a gradual drifting apart. The high school football season that had provided a focus for activities was ending, and the shortening days and the arrival of snow and ice would have made travel up the steep hill to Salinger's house for a record party increasingly difficult. By the late thaw the next season, Salinger could have decided that he should be about what the Vedantic Hinduism he had recently embraced called a "householder's business." The whole episode may be regarded as a fleeting pursuit of the happy pastoral adolescence that Salinger had never known in crowded Manhattan or uptight Valley Forge Military Academy, but his thirty-fifth birthday on 1 January 1954 could have reminded him that time's winged chariot hurried on.

Also in 1953 at a party in the exquisitely fashionable village of Manchester, Vermont (another world from New Hampshire's prosaic metropolis of the same name), seemingly frozen in the graces of the eighteenth century, Salinger had met Claire Douglas, described by the research staff of *Time* magazine, as an "unimpeachably right-looking, extraordinarily pretty" English-born Radcliffe student, who like Franny in Salinger's story,[23] became "hung on the Jesus Prayer." The relationship did not progress smoothly. Claire abruptly broke with Salinger and married a man from the Harvard Business School, but the liaison lasted only a few months before she divorced him and returned to Cornish to wed Salinger on 17 February 1955 at Barnard, Vermont.

Just the month before, "Franny," a serious meditation on the vanity of human wishes and the solace of prayer, had appeared in the *New Yorker* (29 January), Salinger's first new story in two years. It seems difficult not to consider it as his present celebrating the consecration of the wedding, although readers were too busy speculating about Franny's condition at the time of the story (she was not yet identified with the Glass family) to consider this connection, and news of the story traveled faster than news of the nuptials.

In retrospect, we can see that 1955 may have been Salinger's "ripest" year in the Shakespearean sense of the word. It was not until early in the 1950s that Salinger had become interested in Advaita Vedanta, the form of Hinduism that Eberhard Alsen argues persuasively provides the principal theological framework for the "eclectic ideology" of the

Glass family stories.[24] Salinger studied these doctrines formally under Swami Nikhilananda, founder of the Ramakrishna Vivekananda Center in New York City. Salinger became a good friend of the guru and of his successor, Swami Adiswarananda, and has remained associated with the center, attending lectures in recent years and participating in a summer seminar at a retreat in Thousand Island Park.

The Vedantic teachings especially affected "Raise High the Roof Beam, Carpenters," his second story to appear in 1955 (*New Yorker*, 19 November), and the first to introduce Buddy Glass, Seymour's younger brother as narrator. Many readers, like John Updike, feel it is one of Salinger's most attractive and memorable works. This epithalamium, describing the confusing day of Seymour's marriage, was also the last story that Salinger allowed to be anthologized (*Short Stories from the New Yorker, 1950–1960*). It appeared less than a month before the birth of his first child, a daughter, Margaret Ann, on 10 December.

Even more remarkably in this same month of December 1955, Salinger sent for publication in the New York *Post*, a copy of a letter he had written to New York's governor Nelson Rockefeller about the lonely condition of the men sequestered in the state's prisons. If there are any other examples of Salinger's thus volunteering to serve as a kind of national conscience, they have not come to light. Despite his already impressive reputation, the letter was generally ignored.

The dreary election year of 1956 passed with no new word coming down from Read's Hill. Unexpected family responsibilities, acquiring a wife and child within a single year, could certainly have turned upside down the domestic life of one accustomed to nothing more taxing than weekend parties with generally decorous Upper Valley teenagers. When the word arrived in the *New Yorker* for 4 May 1957, it was a shocker, for nothing had prepared a long waiting public for the prolixity, the tediousness, and the finickiness of "Zooey." Besides taking up the problems of Franny (already assimilated into the Glass family in "Raise High the Roof Beam, Carpenters") and presumably solving them, it set forth the concept of the family developed further in the only two stories to follow.

Then, after a two-year silence, Salinger, in "Seymour: An Introduction," which appeared in the 6 June 1959 *New Yorker*, assigned most of his previous writings to stand-in Buddy Glass. Salinger depicted Buddy as living close to New England in upstate New York in an isolation similar to the author's (but without even the phone that Salinger did have, thought unlisted), without any family, but with a job as writer-in-residence at a girl's college somewhat resembling Skidmore.

The problem with "Seymour" has been summarized with elegant and withering precision by John Updike, a fellow protégé of the *New Yorker*, in his brief comment "a lecturer has usurped the writing stand."[25] Updike writes with all the sympathetic admiration that can be expected of one who is less cherished by the "general public" but more at home in the literary establishment.

It is impossible and really improper to investigate whatever personal problems may have turned Salinger from someone resembling Holden Caulfield into someone resembling his tormentor Antolini (and I speak here *only* of Antolini as the long-winded bore). I think, however, that one external literary development does require mention.

Between "Raise High the Roof Beam, Carpenters" in 1955 and "Seymour," the Beats had emerged into the spotlight. Before the uproar over Allen Ginsberg's *Howl* in 1956, Salinger had had the countercultural scene almost entirely to himself; and, something that has been almost totally overlooked in Salinger studies and cannot be overemphasized, is that though Salinger was a critic of mainstream culture through the fifties, he could not be accused of any radical leftist associations or leanings. A member of the counter-intelligence corps in the army, conspicuously apolitical in tendency and with a finicky sensibility that made a British aristocrat (Esmé) his only totally adjusted and admirable character, at home among the very reserved and taciturn residents of upper New England, Salinger must have regarded the "Dharma Bums"that he castigated in "Seymour: An Introduction" with profound distaste. Although he and Allen Ginsberg, for example, both criticized the same dehumanizing tactics of Madison Avenue and sought a spiritual solution to the time's malaise in traditional Eastern religious doctrines, Salinger shunned the spotlight that the Beats courted (to their later remorse) and the psychedelic drug scene. Though his characters smoke too much, they never smoke pot. Salinger was well aware of the impact the Beats were making, but he must have found them virtually unspeakably *vulgar,* another unfortunate development that intensified his desire for privacy and protection for his growing family.

A son, Matthew, was born 13 February 1960, but the marriage lasted only until 1967, when his wife obtained a divorce in Newport, New Hampshire. She and everyone else involved have resolutely refused to discuss either the Salingers' married life or its breakup, but many familiar with the region were surprised that the marriage lasted as long as it did, because, at nearby Dartmouth College, for example, many individuals from sophisticated backgrounds often became depressed and defeated at last by the lonely isolation of the long, dark upper New England winters and the proud provincialism of longtime residents. (Salinger has apparently thrived in this often bleak atmosphere, but he may have expected too much of others.) The children continued to visit Salinger and, after reaching voting age, at times maintained voting residences in Cornish, although they scrupulously avoided the press.

Daughter Margaret Ann has, in fact, continued to avoid publicity as completely as her mother, but son Matthew has recently basked in the limelight that his father shunned by successfully following the very path that once tempted J. D. Salinger himself. While an undergraduate at Columbia University, Matt—as he is now identified—took three acting classes and one singing lesson a week at the Lee Strasberg Institute. This training resulted in some appearances in off-Broadway theaters and led to his starring in *Deadly Deception,* a made-for-television movie, which premiered in CBS 8 March 1987.[26]

Salinger's last published story had appeared in the *New Yorker,* 19 June 1965, before the breakup of his family. "Hapworth 16, 1924" is a story of at least seventeen thousand words in the improbable form of a letter from seven-year-old Seymour Glass to his parents from a summer boarding camp in Maine, during Seymour and his five-year-old brother Buddy's first exile to one of those fashionable establishments that affluent big-city people use to get the kids out of their hair during summer vacations. The letter is remarkable for its exotic vocabulary, Byzantine style, painfully self-conscious psychoanalysis and belletristic standards of literary evaluation. It was not generally well received even by Salinger's large following, and it has never been reprinted.

The Forest Years

Salinger reputedly spends much of his time in a concrete bunker on his hilltop property, where he continues to write works that he refuses to discuss and does not wish to publish. When he moved to Cornish in 1953, he bought a small saltbox house that had been built by John Dodge, the architect-husband of sculptor Augustus Saint-Gaudens's granddaughter Carlota. After the birth of his second child, the family moved across the road to what historian Hugh Mason Wade describes as a "loftier Tyrolean lodge" that Salinger had built on the southern shoulder of Read's Hill, with a view across the Saint-Gaudens National Historic Site and the Connecticut River to Mount Ascutney in Vermont.[27]

To protect his privacy against encroaching new settlers and summer visitors, as well as reporters and adulators seeking rarely granted interviews, he has become a substantial property holder. In 1978, he had the fourth largest private land holdings in the town of Cornish, assessed at $216,350.[28] His desire for privacy is scrupulously respected by his Yankee neighbors, who tend in the tradition of this rocky region to be themselves very private persons, mostly highly traditional members of the historic chapel of the United Church of Christ, modern descendant's of the Puritan congregations that settled the region as a refuge from the decadent world. Since he recieves his mail through Windsor, the original capital of Vermont, across the river, he rarely visits Cornish Flat, the only settlement of any size (about 175 residents) in hilly Cornish, except when he has official business with the efficient and generally affable town clerk, Bernice Mae Fitch Johnson, who steadfastly refuses to talk about him to visitors at the selectmen's office in the town.

Salinger has gradually cut himself off from earlier intimates. Although he wrote a tribute to Whit Burnett in 1965, which Burnett found so effusive that it was not published until after his death, Burnett's efforts to buy two stories, "A Young Man in a Stuffed Shirt" and "The Daughters of the Late Great Man" for a revival of *Story* magazine in 1959 were rejected by an agent; Burnett returned them with regrets that Salinger had not sent a personal note. In 1963, another request to reprint "The Long Debut of Lois Taggett" in a *Story* anthology was denied.[29]

Uninvited callers are discouraged in Cornish. A few have broken through Salinger's physical and psychic barriers to be granted generally uninformative interviews of only a few minutes' duration. The interview inscrutably granted to the persistent Betty Eppes of the *Baton Rouge Advocate* and *State Times*, who had driven up from Louisiana in June 1980, elicited only the information that Salinger ate only organically grown food and used only cold-pressed oil and that he believed in his own version of the American dream, which he refused to explain. The meeting ended disastrously when a third party, a local bookseller intervened in an effort to shake Salinger's hand. Salinger became enraged and blamed Ms. Eppes for a stranger's touching him. "I'm a

private person," she quotes him as saying. "I resent interviews. I resent
questions. I don't want to talk to strangers. I write for myself. For my
own pleasure."[30] She was told not to drop in again, though he later
sent her "an oversized schoolbag from Denmark" and a signed letter.
She described him as having "black eyes that glittered and just seemed
to gaze right out at you," and she made both an unauthorized recording
of their conversation and took some not very satisfactory unauthorized
photographs.[31]

Some people have made the grave mistake, however, of assuming
that because Salinger does not wish to become involved in mundane
affairs, he neither knows nor cares what is going on in the world. Only
such an arrogant presumption could have determined a still unidentified "Greenberg" to undertake a pirated edition of Salinger's uncollected stories that circulated in 1974 in the San Francisco Bay area.
The stories were copied from their original sources (not without some
errors) in the chronological order of their publication on a primitive
model of a typewriter that justifies right margins. They were photo-
copied for binding in two paperback volumes.

The entrepreneur peddled a number of copies to San Francisco booksellers without incident, but when he was emboldened to offer copies
to a prominent New York book mart with an impeccable reputation,
Salinger's agent was informed. Salinger responded by calling Lacey Fosburgh, San Francisco staffer for the *New York Times* to protest the piracy
angrily. In the course of this call, he memorably defined his position
by describing publication as "a terrible invasion of my privacy."[32] A
suit against the offending booksellers was settled in Salinger's favor in
1986.

Similarly when British writer Ian Hamilton undertook to publish in
August 1986 an unauthorized biography of Salinger, based in part on
previously unpublished materials, Salinger again through an agent objected and obtained a restraining order.[33] This temporary order became
a permanent injunction when, in November 1987, the U.S. Supreme
Court refused to review the verdicts of two lower federal appeals courts
that had upheld Salinger's position. The American and British publishers, however, then announced plans to publish a completely re-
drafted book with the title "The Search for Salinger" in 1988.[34]

When a new publisher replaced octogenarian editor William Shawn
of the *New Yorker* in 1987, Salinger joined other longtime contributors
in a letter to the new editor asking that he refuse the post, but some

people objected that Salinger had not contributed to the magazine in so long that it was really none of his business.[35]

He is not a total recluse. He turned up, for example, at a testimonial dinner for the retirement of John L. Keenan, with whom he had served in World War II.[36] Quite possibly he has managed other such trips undetected. He appears to be entirely in control of his affairs; he simply does not want to be bothered. I have seen only one letter that he has written in the last twenty years. It was most courteously worded, but absolutely firm in the refusal to accept a gift from a young admirer of his writings, because such occasions embarrass him. As the incident during the Eppes interview in Windsor suggests, Salinger apparently simply does not want to be involved in any situations that he does not totally control. He has earned the right to mind his own business, and he insists also that others mind theirs.

Others do not always do so; thus Salinger cannot always escape the publicity he shuns. Kevin Sims's documentary, *The Man Who Shot John Lennon*, telecast on British ITV, 2 February 1988, and on 9 February on the American PBS "Frontline" program, dramatized the way in which a misreading of *The Catcher in the Rye* influenced the slaying of the former Beatle by Mark David Chapman, who had totally identified himself with Holden Caulfield.

Chapter Two
Breaking into Print

Bruce Bawer cannot be faulted for his judgment that almost all of Salinger's early stories, "obviously manufactured for a middlebrow audience" in well-paying and widely circulated slick magazines, were contrived productions of little or no literary interest.[1] Salinger is surely adequately justified in his steadfast refusal since 1960 to permit reprintings. Some of these early works, however, have significant relationships to his celebrated later works that merit examination here. Those early stories involved in the curious evolution of the Holden Caulfield character will be examined in connection with *The Catcher in the Rye*.

Salinger's professional literary career begins with his enrolling in Whit Burnett's famous course in short story writing at Columbia University. Burnett's classes served in part to scout out impressive new talents for *Story* magazine, which he edited. Salinger's first published story was written as an assignment for the class.

The *Story* Stories

We cannot be sure of the exact order of composition of the three stories after Salinger's first, "The Young Ones," that appeared in *Story* magazine, or of the date of their compositions in relation to the other twelve stories that he published before his first appearance in the *New Yorker* in 1946. Whit Burnett may have deferred the publication of some early works in order to space out Salinger's contributions to the showcase magazine. Although most of them were published during World War II, only one mentions the war, despite the fact that Salinger had begun to publish other stories with military settings elsewhere as early as 1941. Burnett also did not use in *Story* some other stories with wartime settings that he purchased, one of which is the only story signed "Jerry Salinger."[2] Taken in the order of their publication, however, "The Long Debut of Lois Taggett," "Once a Week Won't Kill

You," and "Elaine" show a shift in their author's sensibility as he gained experience with the genre.

The first accepted and printed story, "The Young Folks," although scarcely more than an unflattering character sketch, remains particularly interesting because of the author's subsequent concern with adolescents. The "young folks" of this story, however, are a very different breed from the protagonists of *The Catcher in the Rye* or some of the "nine stories" like "Just before the War with the Eskimos." They are much more closely related to some of the insensitive schoolmates about whom Holden complains. Salinger's earliest tendency seems to have been to seek to emulate the ironic objective deadpan vignettes of heels found in the popular stories of John O'Hara and Ring Lardner (whom Holden Caulfield admires).

Little happens in the story. Socially ambitious Lucille Henderson has invited a noisy crowd of young people, including Edna Phillips, "to drink up her father's Scotch." Edna spends the evening in a big red chair, eyeing unresponsive young men. Lucille feels obligated to introduce Edna to William Jameson Junior, a compulsive fingernail-biter, who has been staring at Doris Leggett, a small blond girl who is sitting on the floor with three Rutgers students. Edna attempts to strike up a pseudosophisticated conversation with Jameson about a theme he must write on John Ruskin's *Stones of Venice*, but after offering him one of her last three cigarettes during a vain search for Scotch, she switches to bitchy remarks about Doris Leggett and the amorous intentions of a Princeton graduate that she resisted the previous summer. Jameson drifts away and eventually joins the circle around the Leggett girl. When the hostess asks Edna what happened, Edna intimates that the nearly zombielike Jameson made indecent advances toward her. Then she wanders off for twenty minutes into the part of the house supposedly barred to young visitors and returns to resume her red chair, as she extracts "one of ten or twelve cigarettes" from a rhinestone case.[3]

The story is a thoroughly cynical picture of his peers by a twenty-year-old author whose style and vocabulary are still somewhat stilted. At first, it appears that Edna, who seems to display some intellectual interests, is being sympathetically portrayed—like Holden Caulfield—as the victim of a superficial crowd that is fascinated by the phoniness of a bleached blonde, Doris; but Edna turns out to be, if not as empty-headed, even phonier than the rest. The innuendos in her fabricated report of Jameson Junior's behavior cast doubts on everything else she has said, and the climax of the story is not the revelation that she has retired from the party to hide her humiliation at rejection but to search out some cigarettes to pilfer from her hosts.

Salinger already displays here in this first story his remarkable ear for teenage dialogue, but he uses it only for the kind of caricature of the upper crust that also produced on Bob Hope's popular radio programs characters like the outrageous Brenda and Cobina with names borrowed from publicized members of the prewar café society (Cobina Wright, Junior, one of the most conspicuous, could even have suggested Salinger's emphasis in Jameson's peculiar name).[4] The story also illustrates a problem that was to recur in even such much admired later stories as "A Perfect Day for Bananafish" and "Teddy"—the author's demand that the reader pay close attention to seemingly inconsequential details upon which the surprise ending of the stories depends. Unless one recalls that Edna has given one of her last three cigarettes to Jameson, a detail buried in one of the longest paragraphs in this five-thousand-word, largely conversational tale, the importance of the number of cigarettes in Edna's case after she returns from the off-limits family area upstairs is not important. This oversubtlety has led to acrimonious debates over the stories whose resolution depends upon such minute details.

Salinger continued to expose the mendacities of a decadent society only in his second published story, "Go See Eddie," and much later in "Pretty Mouth and Green My Eyes"; but he continued to demonstrate a propensity for O. Henry type surprise endings in the "short, short stories" that were in demand for the "slicks" in the 1930s and 1940s, such as "The Hang of It" and "Personal Notes of an Infantryman."

His second contribution to *Story,* "The Long Debut of Lois Taggett," shows, however, a drift toward sentimentality. The tale suffers from serious structural problems, since the surprise ending turns out to be too much of a surprise, quite inadequately foreshadowed. Lois Taggett comes from the same social set as the characters in "The Young Folks," but displays no more despicable characteristic than irresponsibility. She quits a job as a receptionist that her uncle had arranged for her during "the first big year for debutantes to Do Something" because she prefers to join friends on a cruise to Rio.

She later falls in love just as irresponsibly with a man her family cannot accept because he is a press agent. He later proves also to be a psychotic who, as the narrator puts it, "did what he had to do" when he burns Lois's hand with his cigarette. A week later he smashes her foot with a golf club. After the divorce, he spots her at the Stork Club and tells her that his psychiatrist says he will be all right, but she refuses to resume their relationship. Instead she marries a "dope" named Carl Curfman, whom she makes wear colored socks though they irritate his feet. They have not been married three months when she starts spending all her time going to movies and shopping without finding anything to buy. She changes her ways, however, when she becomes pregnant, but then she begins to cry in her sleep, unnoticed by Carl.

Four paragraphs from the end of this meandering tale, the reader is informed, "Then finally she made it," with the result that people begin to like her. This happens, we are subsequently informed, six months after the "darling" baby dies of what is known now as sudden infant death syndrome. One night as Lois watches the husband she does not love, looking "more stupid and gross" than ever, she suddenly says something she "had to say to him, 'Put on your white socks, dear.'"[5]

The point of contrasting these two incompatible marriages would seem to be that the death of Lois's baby forces her to develop some consideration for other people's feelings that she had not been able to develop in dealing with her first disturbed husband. The problem is that there is no evidence that Lois could possibly have dealt with her first husband's psychosis through a thoughtful gesture (his behavior resembles Seymour Glass's enigmatic throwing of a rock at Charlotte Mayhew during their childhood). She is described as madly in love with him, and there is no intimation that he is in any conscious way seeking revenge of some kind on her. One would want something more than a psychiatrist's guess before getting involved again with such an individual. If the point is that the episode led Lois to distrust love to the extent that she would marry a man she found disagreeable, she would seem to need a psychiatrist herself. Perhaps a person might behave as Lois does in the story, but it is not enough for the writer just to tell us she did; he has to make the actions believable. At key points in this story, Salinger simply shirks an author's responsibilities. We never learn why the first husband behaved as he did, or why Lois had to say to her second husband what she did when she "made it." Yet Whit Burnett not only used "Long Debut" in *Story,* but reprinted it in an anthology and offered to reprint it again—a success that could have encouraged Salinger to pursue the history of such an unlikely pairing as Seymour Glass and Muriel Fedder. The important thing about the tale is that Salinger is here abandoning the fashionable irony of his first published story and displaying a determination to make things work out from a sentimental point of view, even if the result strains credibility—a tendency that many critics later found troubling in the Glass family stories.

Salinger's last two contributions to *Story* bear little relationship to his later works and appear to be exercises in working up character sketches of unworldly types that were not to concern him subsequently. "Once a Week Won't Kill You" reproduces the last conversations with his wife and aunt of a young man about to enter the wartime army. Attention is called twice in a manner unusual in Salinger's writings to the exact date of the action as March 1944 (the year the story was published), though the events seem more likely to have occurred during the confused period right after Pearl Harbor than in the months before D day, when most draftable men had already been drafted. The editors may have been attempting to update a story that had been around for a while.

The title of the story derives from the husband's insistence that, while he is away, his wife take his aunt, who lives in the same apartment building, to the movies once in a while. She agrees without enthusiasm, but she does agree, so there is no real conflict in the story. The aunt (in her early fifties), whom the narrator describes as having an "intelligent face," proves to be as "*batty*" as the young wife suggests, when she gives the nephew a letter of introduction to a friend who died while serving as an army lieutenant in World War I. The nephew, however, regards her as "the sanest woman in the world," because she is not panicked by his reluctant revelation that he has been called into the service.[6] The oversolicitous concern of the nephew who resembles Salinger himself ("I mean you even hate to *talk* to people and everything," his wife observes) turns what could have been a touching situation into a maudlin account of preserving "nice" fantasies no matter how bizarre. Undoubtedly during World War II, in the face of international madness, such excesses were considered morale building; but *Story* seems to have been encouraging Salinger's tendency to mold a hard shell around a gooey center.

An even more bizarre flight from reality provides the climax of "Elaine," a long, episodic tale about a beautiful girl who is mentally retarded. Although the story, Salinger's last in *Story*, did not appear until 1945, there is no mention of the war or the draft in it. It seems set during the depression when Henry Fonda was becoming a matinee idol in films like *Jezebel* and *Jesse James,* and sixty-five dollars a week was a salary that commanded enormous respect. After dwelling to no particular purpose on the scholastic shortcomings of the title character who won two Beautiful Child contests, the story suddenly takes off in an unforeseen direction when Elaine at seventeen marries a young movie usher, with whom she had had her first date only a month earlier. The marriage is never consummated, however, because during the wedding reception Elaine's mother gets into a violent controversy with the groom's mother over the virility of a popular movie star and commands Elaine to leave her husband and come away with her and her grandmother. (The latter has lived with them since Elaine's father dropped dead while watching an indoor flea circus when she was a small child.) After observing that her symbolically drooping corsage was "*so beautiful*," Elaine skips ecstatically back into mother and grandmother's world of radio soap operas and romantic movies where she has already spent most of her youth. There is no hint of sarcasm in the narrator's leaving the impression that she has chosen the best of all possible worlds.

Into and Out of *The Saturday Evening Post*

Salinger began his short and not very happy association with Curtis Publishing's well-paying and widely circulated *Saturday Evening Post* in 1943 with "The Varioni Brothers." This story is the most interesting of his wartime fables because it features his first impressive use of the kind of first-person narrator that he later used to great success. Salinger even had hopes that this story might be sold to the movies (possibly as a vehicle for Henry Fonda).[7] The war does not intrude on this tale, however, as it is set back in the 1920s, which Salinger sees not as a glamorous period, but, probably influenced by *The Great Gatsby,* as "high, wide and rotten."

Prompted by the withering satire and convoluted style of a guest gossip columnist "raconteur" Vincent Westmoreland, who reports on doings "Around Old Chi with Gardenia Penny," Sarah Daley Smith, a teacher at Waycross College in Illinois, answers the question "Where is Sonny Varioni?" with an account of what happened to this popular song writer of the twenties after a gambler's trigger man accidentally shot his lyricist brother Joe by mistake. Sonny had been missing for seventeen years when he turned up at the Waycross College English department, where brother Joe had once taught while writing a novel. The kernel of Sarah's sad tale is that Joe dreamed of being a novelist, but Sonny insisted that he keep writing the lyrics for the songs that were making them famous, for he had no confidence in Joe's succeeding as a fiction writer. Belatedly he decided to come back to Waycross and try to put Joe's novel together, as he explains, "because I hear the music for the first time in my life when I read his book."[8]

The most interesting of Sarah's comments, however, is that to tell the story, she must go back to "the high, wide and rotten Twenties." "I can offer no important lament or even a convincing shrug for the general bad taste of the era," she affirms. The vehemence of the speech that Salinger assigns to her may shed light on Holden Caulfield and Buddy Glass's enormous enthusiasm for Fitzgerald's "old sport" Jay Gatsby, a brilliant, sensitive man like Joe Varioni, who was corrupted and destroyed by a rotten era.

Salinger's next exercise for the *Post,* "Both Parties Concerned," shows an increasing command of first-person narration. Twenty-year-old husband Billy sounds very much like a slightly older Holden Caulfield, even down to his favorite locutions ("we came right home and all"), but his opening caution, "There really isn't too much to tell" proves only too true.[9] Friends had said that he and seventeen-year-old Ruthie, who gives up her ambition to become a doctor for him, are too young to marry. Their skepticism seems justified when Billy wants to go out partying every night, while Ruth wants to stay home with her baby. When she leaves him, however, he sees the error of his ways; and in an unconvincing reconciliation, reminiscent of the forced ending of "The Long Debut of Lois Taggett," husband tells wife that she can wake him up any time the thunder frightens her.

Salinger contributed three more stories to the *Post* before the end of the war, two of which are third-person narratives related to the development of the Holden Caulfield character. The remaining experiment with first-person narration, "Soft-Boiled Sergeant," was less successful than the other two because the language of the regular army enlisted man who tells the sad story of a heroic sergeant who never wins the girl of his dreams because he is physically ugly sounds more like the sanitized speech of *Post* readers than the salty twang of longtime soldiers.

Salinger's finickiness had already led to the first of his problems with insensitive publishers. He complained in April 1944 that he was through with the "slick" magazines because the *Post* had changed titles and illustrated his stories.[10] Whit Burnett had apparently humored his touchy protégé, but the tougher-minded editors of the *Post* were more concerned about readers' tastes than authors'.

Writing for Women's Magazines

After being discharged from the army, Salinger ceased publishing in the popular weeklies, but he contributed four stories to respected women's magazines before establishing his longtime association with the *New Yorker*. Although two of these stories appeared after "A Perfect Day for Bananafish," lead times for publication in monthlies are often far longer than for weeklies and similarities between the three shorter stories of this group suggest that they were all written during the same period before the creation of Seymour Glass.

"A Young Girl in 1941 with No Waist at All" (*Mademoiselle*, May 1947), "A Girl I Knew" (*Good Housekeeping*, February 1948), and "Blue Melody" (*Cosmopolitan*, September 1948) are quite similar in their nostalgic tone and marked departures from the mawkishly sentimental tales that Salinger had turned out during the war. All portray situations that are genuinely pathetic in tones of regret over lost innocence that mount to outrage. All also include scenes derived from Salinger's experiences and develop around a character who in some ways resembles him. In the last two stories this figure serves as the first-person narrator.

Whereas the principal female characters in many of Salinger's earlier stories had been tough, superficial women who posed problems for naive men, "girls" in these three stories are all particularly vulnerable persons, two of them members of persecuted minorities, whom the men looking back into the past recall with disillusioned regret. Salinger may have been deliberately aiming at this point in his career at the lucrative market for fiction women's magazines then afforded (as they still do to a more modest extent), but he may also have simply been experimenting with kinds of stories that the editors of these magazines found particularly appealing to readers who had not found the postwar world all that they had hoped it might be. The stories seem the work of a very serious young writer, back from disillusioning wartime experiences and seeking to get firmly established in a perilous profession, ransacking his own past for realistic tales that closely resembled in sensibility the dark and depressing *films noirs* to which Hollywood producers turned extensively in the late 1940s to try to hold mature audiences that were drifting away from the movie houses they had attended in record numbers during the war. Whatever the motivations behind this group of stories, Salinger did not find in them the theme he pursued in the future, that of a talented, innocent man destroyed by a coldly designing woman.

"A Young Girl" is a comparatively artless story that sees Salinger reverting back to the techniques used in "The Long Debut of Lois Taggett" in order to make a fresh start with somewhat more mature characters. Most of the stories that he wrote during the war had begun to blend into the Holden Caulfield story that would soon take the final form it had been moving toward since his preoccupation with troubled urban youth in "The Young Folks."

Ray Kinsella, a Yale dropout from Kansas City, who serves as an entertainment director on a Caribbean cruise ship, as Salinger had, and who somewhat resembles Hollywood actor Ross Alexander ("a boy who was in a lot of West Pointy pictures with Dick Powell and Ruby Keeler"),[11] as Salinger does in early publicity photos, is the focal character in the story. It is narrated, however, in the third person by an unidentified voice that unnecessarily complicates the tale by including a lot of soap opera material about a wealthy, middle-aged couple who are depressed by the war. Finally, since it has not been clear what is really the main stream of the tangled tale, it is necessary for the narrator to conclude with the ponderous statement that "the fragile hour was a carrier of many things, but Barbara [the young girl of the title] was now exclusively susceptible to the difficult counterpoint sounding just past the last minutes of her girlhood."[12]

Although looking back, the reader can figure out how the marriage proposal she has received from Ray Kinsella (while she is traveling with her fiancé's mother following an illness) might have brought life's complexities home to her, especially at a time when the world was plunging more deeply into war (both men in her life are planning to enter the service and even the cruise ship is to be converted into a troopship), here as in "Lois Taggett," the narrator is obliged finally to tell the readers something that he has not made us see sufficiently clearly for ourselves.

Salinger is more successful in handling a much more complicated tale-within-a-tale in "Blue Melody," which relates in flashback the story of a black singer, Lida Louise Jones, in Memphis. (The account closely resembles the legendary events that led to the death of Bessie Smith of peritonitis when she was refused admission to a white hospital after her appendix burst; Edward Albee presents another version of this shocking incident in his short play "The Death of Bessie Smith.") Lida Louise's death, however, is not the central subject of Salinger's story. The events connected with it are related in flashback by a young man named Rudford from Agersburg, Tennessee, who tells the story of what can certainly be described as the last minutes of his boyhood to an unidentified narrator as they are riding in an army truck from Luxembourg to the warfront in Germany.

Rudford and his girlfriend Peggy had been the youngest members of an enthusiastic audience when Lida Louise had sung at her uncle Black Charles's nightclub in Agersburg, though they had had to sneak to this forbidden establishment on Miss Paula's Street and keep their admiration for the singer secret. They are on a farewell picnic with the singer and her relatives before Rudford's departure for boarding school when the fatal attack occurs. Rudford never returns to Agersburg, but he meets Peggy again fifteen years later during the war. She is married to a Navy flier, who is bored by her and Rudford's reminiscences about Lida Louise. In a scene in the Biltmore Hotel bar Peggy reveals that one of their former white classmates is now living on a gentrified Miss Paula's street. A drunk smashed Peggy's copy of Lida Louise's famous recording of "Soupy Peggy," which the Varioni brothers had written for her (this unique link between two early Salinger stories suggests he may have projected a group of downbeat tales about jazz musicians), and Peggy has not heard it since. Rudford tells her he has one and will arrange for her to hear it, but he never does, nor does he see her again—"he almost never played that record for *any*body in 1942."

Rudford's alienation suggests the meaning of a curious passage at the beginning of the story, in which the unnamed narrator explains that the story tells all he knows about Rudford and that the story is not "a slam against one section of the country." "It isn't a slam against anybody or anything," he maintains. "It's just a simple little story of Mom's apple pie, ice-cold beer, the Brooklyn Dodgers, and the Lux Theater of the Air—the things we fought for, in short."[13] Rudford's story seems to justify even more then *The Catcher in the Rye* William Faulkner's comment on Holden Caulfield, "his tragedy was not that he was, as he perhaps thought, not tough enough or brave enough or deserving enough to be accepted into humanity. His tragedy was that when he attempted to enter the human race, there was no human race there."[14] Faulkner probably never heard of "Blue Melody," since it has not been resurrected from the unlikely pages of *Cosmopolitan*; but it would be interesting to know his reaction to this visitor's story of the region he knew so well. (Salinger was apparently in Tennessee only for a brief period early in his military service; Rudford's father in the story is a northerner, who marries a southern girl, but moves off to San Francisco after her death.) Since Salinger's handling of the narrator's opening statement is heavy-handed, readers have generally missed the point that the story is not just another attack on racism in the South, but a world-weary man's metaphorical explanation of his disillusionment with his own culture.

Salinger is more successful in making a similar point in "A Girl I Knew,"; although on the rare occasions they have examined the story, critics have condemned Salinger for being too soft on the villains. The story well deserves, however, its selection for Martha J. Foley's *Best American Short Stories of 1949*. Even though Salinger disdains such honors, the collection keeps this deserving example of Salinger's early work more easily available than many of the others.

The story simply relates some incidents that could have been drawn from Salinger's own experiences when, after graduating from Valley Forge Military Academy, he was sent abroad to study in Vienna and Poland. The events are presented without much comment, so that the readers can work out for themselves what they mean.

After flunking out of college in 1936 (when Salinger left the military school) eighteen-year-old, six-foot-two, 119-pound John is sent to Vienna and Paris "to learn a couple of languages" for his father's business. In Vienna, he becomes acquainted with a young Jewish girl, who lives in the same apartment house. They spend a number of evenings together in his apartment, holding idle conversations during which he practices his bad German and she her bad English. "We just never said anything to each other," he reports. He learns by accident that she is engaged to a young Pole and thinks that this may account for her disinclination to meet him away from home, but he also speculates that he may just be worrying too much or hesitating "to risk letting the thing we had together deteriorate into a romance."[15] He thinks he used to know, but he feels that he does not any longer.

Leah is in Warsaw visiting her fiancé's family when John leaves for Paris. She writes once to send him two American records that their now dead landlady wanted him to have, but she does not give her married name or address. In 1940, John meets a Viennese girl who went through school with Leah, but she is more interested in talking about "a man in Philadelphia, who looked exactly like Gary Cooper," and can only tell him that "Leah either had got out of Vienna or hadn't got out of Vienna" at the time of the German takeover. While in the army in Europe after the war, John has to deliver some papers to Vienna and inquires from former neighbors about Leah. He is directed to a Doctor Weinstein who has just come back to Vienna from the Buchenwald concentration camp.

John's interview with the doctor is not shared with readers; instead we go with John to the apartment house where he had lived. There, despite agonizing difficulties with a red-haired army staff sergeant of the same breed as Corporal Clay in "For Esmé—with Love and Squalor," John manages to get back into his old apartment to look down at the balcony where he had first seen Leah. He observes that "nothing in the room had been there in 1936." He does not need to say that you cannot repeat the past. There is so much of it that one would not care to repeat.

"The Inverted Forest"

Wandering back into "The Inverted Forest" after twenty-five years of at least annual visits to *The Catcher in the Rye* and *Nine Stories* is not a much happier experience than the soldier's return to his former Vienna apartment in "A Girl I Knew." The story of an incredibly talented poet (Ray Ford) who cannot stand the attention of admirers, including a devoted wife (Corinne), has few redeeming features. His fatal attraction to a scheming woman (Bunny) who reminds him of his mother fails to move the reader. None of the characters is plausible as the allegorical demigods they seem to be (the wounded poet, the benevolent patron, the destructive witch). One wonders what attracted a fashionable magazine like *Cosmopolitan* to such a highbrow work, which has passing allusions to T. S. Eliot, at a time when Salinger's name was not yet one that sold magazines (although one can understand what prompted the magazine to fight to keep his name on the cover of its diamond jubilee issue in 1961 when the convoluted tale seemed worlds away from the bathroom realism of the just collected *Franny and Zooey*). The year of 1947, however, when "The Inverted Forest" appeared was also the year that Tennessee Williams's play *A Streetcar Named Desire* scored an enormous success, following up his *Glass Menagerie* (1944) as a revelation of the tragedy of the destruction of the oversensitive wounded at the hands of a gross world. Truman Capote was shortly to continue this trend with great success in *Other Voices, Other Rooms* (1948) and other early stories. Fleur Cowles was shortly to launch her pretentious journal *Flair,* in the first issue of which Charles J. Rolo celebrated the return of the literary salon by revealing that "there are relatively few strongholds of the New York aristocracy which [had] not succumbed to the attractions of today's de luxe Bohemia."[16] Those who expected Salinger to join the coterie producing the literature of preciosity, however, were doomed to early disappointment, although Rolo's effusions may provide a clue to what Salinger was fleeing when admirers of Capote's *The Grass Harp* got hold of *The Catcher in the Rye.*

In my earlier book about Salinger, I lavished space on some fanciful theories about "The Inverted Forest" as an oblique rejection—like Hart Crane's—of T. S. Eliot's disenchanted view of modern world as a wasteland, based on the only two lines quoted from the two volumes of poetry by Ford who is described by another character as "Coleridge and Blake and Rilke all in one, and more"—"Not wasteland, but a great inverted forest . . . with all foliage underground."[17] Now it does not seem worth spending time on a story that has impressed few readers.

Ford, however, has just enough similarities to Seymour Glass and even Salinger himself that one cannot pretend that the work never happened, especially since it was Salinger's longest work to date (around forty thousand words) at a critical point in his career. He was casting about for ways to establish himself in the shrinking post–World War II literary market, before "A Perfect Day for Bananafish" and *The Catcher in the Rye* unexpectedly earned him a preeminent place, allowing him to set trends instead of follow them. "The Inverted Forest" does appear to be a false start toward the creation of Seymour Glass, whom Salinger would have brother Buddy describe as deserving to stand with the "only three or four *very* nearly non-expendable poets" in this century (*Seymour,* 157).

Lest I was overreacting negatively after a long-deferred return visit, I checked to see what others have said about the work. Observing that it was "dispiriting" to find that Salinger could print "The Inverted Forest" a year after the first Holden Caulfield story in the *New Yorker,* Frederick L. Gwynn and Joseph L. Blotner in their pioneering pamphlet appraising Salinger included a summary of its irredeemably fantastic plot only to lead to the unanswered question, "What *is* significant about what *has* happened?"[18]

Kenneth Hamilton makes more sense of the story than anyone else I have encountered; but, on careful examination, his comment that Ford's first wife, Corinne "appreciates his genius but expects him to lead a normal married life with her, while his second wife, Bunny, . . . destroys him as a man, but through her strong-willed self absorption, gives him liberty to develop the inner springs of poetic creativity"[19] does not hold up, for Corinne makes no demands on him, and he is never married to the adulterous Bunny, who does not understand his poetry but is interested only in something that will make money.

Paul Levine gets the point of the story when he observes that Ford "returns to the miserable state of his childhood when he saw neither poetry nor the real world" and that Salinger's insight into his dilemma is that, like Holden and Seymour, Ford is a misfit who can never be accepted by, or accept, society and that Bunny is "as immoral as the bed-hopping heroine of 'Pretty Mouth and Green My Eyes.'"[20] Levine leaves hapless readers, however, with the impression that the story might be worth digging out as a contribution to Salinger's picture of "the corrupt, materialistic, loveless world of the grown-up where adult and adultery are synonymous," because he misses what may be the key line of the story, which is buried amid a vast amount of claptrap in Ford's first conversation with childhood supporter Corinne when they are reunited after nineteen years. Explaining that he does not smoke or drink, he continues "I still think that, in a way, I can't get past half my childhood dogmas" (118). This is one of the most obvious half-truths in fiction, because what the story reveals is that he cannot get past any of them. He is as hopelessly frozen in his childhood as the Indians in the Museum of Natural History in *The Catcher in the Rye* are frozen in their diorama—a condition that Salinger seems to suppose necessary for the cultivation of poetic genius. When Corinne asks Ford to leave Bunny and come home, he refuses, explaining briefly, "I'm with the Brain again," then adds, "*You* saw the original. Think back. Think of somebody pounding on the window of a restaurant on a dark street" (132). He is referring to his mother.

How does this frightening picture of permanently arrested development relate to the rest of Salinger's work? Bruce Bawer, in his review of Ian Hamilton's uncirculated biography, complains about its lack of information (through no fault of Hamilton's) about the childhood of a writer "whose fiction is enigmatically obsessed with the theme of childhood—whose entire *oeuvre* cries out for a biographer able to shed some light on the reasons for its strange fixation."[21] Bawer then goes on to try to affix the responsibility himself on the bitchiness of bourgeois New York society, asking whether Salinger, "born into a family that lived on a modest block of upper Broadway," felt "out of place in the Park Avenue apartment that his family moved into when he was thirteen? Did the other young men in his New York set, most of whom presumably had been born into their wealth, intimidate him?" (39).

Bawer may, because of dogmas of his own, be missing the point. The one issue that characters in Salinger's fiction never show the slightest sense of uneasiness about is their place in society. The lower class is depicted in *The Catcher in the Rye* with withering disdain; and even though Holden loathes his flashy roommate Stradtlater, he rooms with him because "at least his suitcases were as good as mine" (142). The idea that seems firmly fixed in Salinger's mind is the Wordsworthian one that children come into the world "trailing clouds of glory." Once grown to manhood, as the Bible warns, one sees "through a glass darkly." Even though Holden reconciles himself to kids growing up and grabbing for the gold ring, they do so at the price of losing the ability to see God face to face.

It is the responsibility of the world to encourage these fleeting gifts at the earliest possible age, as we cannot expect the gifted like Seymour and Teddy to survive long in a world, in which, as T. S. Eliot put it in "Gerontion," "What is kept must be adulterated." If one's "lousy childhood" discourages the development of one's natural gifts, one may be handicapped all one's life. The most curious feature of Salinger's obsession with childhood is his vision of having all seven of the Glass children successively dominate a children's quiz program that Seymour even manages to turn into a kind of public forum for the children's views. (This kind of radio program did not actually even exist until 1940.)[22] What seems to have bothered Salinger as child is that adults did not listen to him (a view that is also suggested by seven-year-old Seymour's attitude toward his mother and father in "Hapworth 16, 1924"). I doubt that anyone ever intimidated Salinger at any age; he was much more likely annoyed that they did not pay attention to what he said.

The point of "The Inverted Forest" seems most likely to be that a child's precious talents may be wasted if they are not nurtured early, even though they may enjoy some late flowering. Raymond Ford is never going to be able to adjust to even a modest celebrity life in New York; his evil genius has found him out and condemned him to slaving away, turning out kitsch in a midwestern tenement. "The Inverted Forest" is indeed "dispiriting" in more ways than Gwynn and Blotner meant when they first made this comment; it is a curious work for Salinger to have composed just before his success with the Seymour Glass and Holden Caulfield stories, and it is not surprising that he wrote nothing more in this vein and sought to prevent a republication of this tale about an artist's sad fate, one that he himself escaped.

Chapter Three
The Holden Caulfield Story

Back in his talkative days just after World War II, Salinger told Herschel Brickell that he might never finish a novel, because he was "essentially a short story writer" and did not want to abuse his talent or spread it too thin.[1] He did go on, however, to finish just one; and it went on to become what Bruce Bawer calls "perhaps the best known story in postwar American literature."[2]

The Evolution of Holden Caulfield

The novel did not mark the beginning of a phase in the author's career, but the end of perhaps his only successful one (depending on one's enthusiasm for the Glass family stories to follow). Salinger had been shaping the character of a young man hard pressed by the world for a long time, probably from the beginning of his determined efforts to become a writer back at Valley Forge Military Academy, for he did tell Shirley Blaney that his "boyhood was very much the same "as that of the boy in his book."[3] Only a year after Salinger's professional debut in *Story,* he achieved an accolade few apprentice writers could anticipate, when a story about Holden Caulfield was accepted by the *New Yorker*; but alas, the attack on Pearl Harbor followed too close on this acceptance, and the story was shelved for the duration.

An updated version, "Slight Rebellion Off Madison" appeared in a postwar Christmas issue (21 December 1946). In the meantime, however, Salinger had not shelved the character. Salinger mentioned to Whit Burnett in 1942 that he was already at work on a novel about a boy, although he later wrote that he had had to quit working on it during his service in the army.[4] William Maxwell later reported that in 1946, however, Salinger had completed a ninety-page novelette version of *The Catcher in the Rye,* which a publisher was willing to accept, but which the dissatisfied author decided to do over again.[5] Unfortunately, the evolution of the character is impossible to follow, because neither the original version of the short story nor the shorter version of the novel has been made public; and it is not likely that either will be.

Maxwell, however, who had seen the earlier version, wrote that the final book was "much richer, much deeper, more subjective, and more searching."

Salinger had, however, in the meantime killed off the original Holden Caulfield in some published stories, in which a figure with the same name, who strikingly resembles the hero of the novel, is reported missing in action during World War II. (Actually this Holden's death is never confirmed, but if he had survived he would have been too old to return as an adolescent in a novel mentioning events that occurred in 1949.) Soldier Holden's brother Vincent, who is himself reported in "The Stranger" to have been meaninglessly killed in action late in the war, spends his time in "Last Day of the Last Furlough" and "This Sandwich Has No Mayonnaise" moping over reports that the brother he describes as "the noisiest, tightest kid in the old Joe College Club on Eighteenth and Third in New York,"[6] is missing in action.

In "Last Day of the Last Furlough," it is reported also that Holden would have been twenty years old in December 1943 (the date is not supplied in the story, but in "A Boy in France," Babe Gladwaller, the principal character is both tales, receives a letter dated 5 July 1944 after having been shipped overseas following the furlough described in the other story). Holden would thus have been an appropriate age to be the principal character in the story the *New Yorker* bought in 1941. This Holden's history is further confused because in "This Sandwich Has No Mayonnaise," Vincent's brother, who had been missing in action in 1943, is said to have "come through the war in Europe without a scratch" and to have been shipped out to the Pacific, where he is reported missing in action, in 1945. This development could only have been the result of an authorial or editorial update, however, since Vincent is depicted in this story as being at a camp in Georgia before being sent overseas in 1943. It is not clear, in fact, why *Esquire* published such a story at all in October 1945, after the end of the war; but in view of a monthly's need to prepare its layout weeks in advance of the month of publication, the story may already have been in press when the Japanese surrendered. However, none of this really matters much any more since Salinger has understandably made every effort to keep these wartime Babe Gladwaller stories out of subsequent circulation, and the original Holden, whom we never actually meet in person, has been definitively replaced by his postwar avatar.

One value that the stories do have, however, is that they disprove the theory fondly accepted even by Bruce Bawer, following Ian Hamilton, that supposed movie-hater Salinger named his character for two screen stars, William Holden and Joan Caulfield. While Holden, one of the postwar superstars, had indeed made his much ballyhooed debut as *Golden Boy* in 1939 in time to provide his somewhat common name for the figure, the more unusually named Caulfield did not begin her shorter and less spectacular career until she debuted in *Miss Susie Slagle's* in February 1946, almost two years after Holden Caulfield was first named in print in "Last Day of the Last Furlough," at a time when Salinger already had a novelette about him being considered for publication.

A character named Holden Caulfield who does have some of the same experiences as the narrator of *The Catcher in the Rye* appears in *Collier's* 1945 Christmas issue in a short story called "I'm Crazy" and reappears in the *New Yorker's* 1946 Christmas issue in "Slight Rebellion Off Madison"; but events repeated in the novel from these stories are portrayed in the novel as occurring during Christmas week in 1949. The dates of the action in "Slight Rebellion Off Madison" and *Catcher* are unmistakably established in the account of Holden's taking Sally Hayes to a Broadway theater to see Alfred Lunt and Lynn Fontanne: in the short story the narrator summarizes a play that is unmistakably *O Mistress Mine,* which opened in February 1946, so that the action of the story seems contemporaneous with its publication; in the novel Holden satirizes the plot of *I Know My Love,* which opened in the fall of 1949.

William Maxwell's comment that *The Catcher in the Rye* is more subjective than the 1946 novelette version is particularly arresting, because a principal difference between the 1946 *New Yorker* story, "Slight Rebellion Off Madison," and the novel is that the former is written in the third person, so that it lacks the poignancy and immediacy of the final version's first-person narration. Salinger, however, had been experimenting with his approach to his material even before the *New Yorker* story appeared, because "I'm Crazy," which contains material used later in *Catcher,* is narrated by Holden himself at the time of his expulsion from what was then called "Pentey Prep." Holden has not been expelled in "Slight Rebellion Off Madison"; he has just come home on Christmas vacation, bearing a middle name "Morrisey" that never turns up anywhere again.

The Holden Caulfield*s* and *the* Holden Caulfield

Whatever the incalculable significance of the suppression of this middle name may be, its revelation brings us to the question of how to account for the phenomenal popularity of Salinger's single novel, but first we must consider what little we know of the development of the tale that the disturbed narrator unfolds.

The first quarter of the novel moves through seven chapters at a deceptively leisurely pace, as Holden tries to figure out how to face a double crisis. He had been expelled from Pencey Prep, a self-styled character-molding institution, after having experienced difficulties trying to adjust himself to several other private boys' boarding schools, and he has been ostracized by the fencing team that he manages for losing its equipment on a New York subway. He is more disturbed by his peers' rejection than by his academic failure.

"People never notice things," he complains.[7] Many readers have in fact not noticed that as a result of growing six and one half inches in six months and nearly developing TB, Holden is physically as well as psychically ill. Another matter overlooked by readers caught up by the hypnotic rhythm of Holden's monologue is that it is quite odd that Pencey Prep is playing the final football game of the season against its traditional rival the week before the Christmas recess, though school and college football seasons usually end Thanksgiving weekend. In "I'm Crazy"—in which the school is called Pentey—it is much more realistically playing basketball on a December evening; but Salinger had dramatic reasons for wanting to move the sporting event to the afternoon in order to provide time for more disheartening encounters between Holden and his suitemates before he sets out on the lonely midnight journey he decides he must make.

Also before Holden leaves, he must make an especially depressing visit to his history teacher, who plays on Holden the "dirty trick" of making the boy listen to a stupid test answer he has written; then when Holden provides Old Spencer with the opportunity to be sympathetic by wistfully observing that he may just be going through a phase, the teacher mutters that he just does not know, though he has had a lifetime to watch boys go through phases. (In "I'm Crazy," Holden tells the teacher that he has no "plans," because he just lives "day by day.")

A significant difference between the novel and the earlier short story is that, whereas in "I'm Crazy," as the title indicates, Holden repeatedly puts the blame for what has happened on his own inadequacies, in the novel he shifts the blame to the "morons" he encounters. The deprecatory description of himself as "crazy" in the story indicates Holden's acceptance of an external conventional standard to which he cannot measure up—it is a defeatist admission of inferiority due to abnormality. In the novel, Holden's blanket use of "morons" to describe others indicates a contemptuous condescension toward the failure of his society to measure up to *his* expectations. The shift is one of the techniques that enabled Salinger to charm readers of the novel who identify with Holden by assuring them of their inherent superiority.

In "I'm Crazy" Holden also speaks of his sister Phoebe and an even younger sister Viola (becoming acquainted with her is the principal reason readers may still enjoy going back to the short story) as "one of us," part of what Jean-Luc Godard in a French new wave tough-guy "losers" film of the early 1960s called "a band of outsiders" (*bande à part*); but at the end of *Catcher* Holden dismisses the question of whether he is going to "apply himself" as "stupid" and speaks messianically of the way that *he* has begun to miss everyone, even "scraggly bums" like the bellyboy Maurice. Somewhere between 1945 and 1951, Salinger dramatically changed his concept of his misfit hero from that of a pathetically misunderstood person who felt a need to apologize for himself and seemed doomed to an undistinguished life in New York's wasteland to that of one who has learned to transcend the morons and show his compassion for them by generous gestures.[8] Holden does sometimes in *Catcher* speak of himself as a "madman," but even this term implies a kind of superiority, someone who is more a threat to the world than its victim. It is probably a sense of this condescension on Holden's part that has upset conformist critics of the novel even if they have not been able to articulate their discomfort and have sought a scapegoat in the objectionable language that also expresses a threat to polite society.

Also conspicuously strengthened from the scenes repeated from the short story is a key passage in Holden's conversation with Phoebe when he visits her before confronting their parents. When Phoebe complains in "I'm Crazy" that Holden "doesn't like *anything*," he can only come up with the evasive reply, "I like girls I haven't met yet; girls that you can just see the back of their heads, a few seats ahead of you on the train"—the kind of conventional daydreaming reply one might expect in a slick magazine story.[9] Nothing here matches Holden's vivid vision, which gives the novel its title and also casts Holden in a messianic role as both judge and policeman. There is nothing in the short story to

counter the impression that Holden is never going to amount to anything; in the novel, however, Holden fantasizes himself into an almost
Superman-like figure who would be the nemesis of evildoers if he only
had the guts. Somewhere along the road to publication and unexpected
super-success, Salinger had decided that his hero did not have to be
defeated by the world, though he might not be able to defeat it. There-
after his fiction becomes a search for escape routes from the maddening
crowd.

Although "Slight Rebellion Off Madison" appeared a year after "I'm
Crazy," the Holden Morrisey Caulfield who appears in it cannot be
reconciled with either the Holden in the earlier story or the later novel.
It seems quite likely that "I'm Crazy" comes from the 1946 manuscript
that William Maxwell mentions, while "Slight Rebellion Off Madison"
is an updating of the story that the *New Yorker* accepted in 1941.
Rather than a misfit, he is, quite incongruously in view of what happens in the story, a nattily dressed young man about town. The third-
person narrative does, however, contain one passage that is repeated
almost exactly in the novel, bringing out the one enduring trait in
Holden's shifting characterizations. At the Radio City ice-skating rink,
where Holden and Sally Hayes go after attending a play starring the
Lunts, their hitherto playful dalliance takes a serious turn when Holden asks, "Do you like school?" Sally replies:

> "It's a terrific bore."
> "Do you hate it, I mean?"
> "Well, I don't hate it."
> "Well, *I* hate it," said Holden. "Boy, do I hate it."[10]

He then goes into a now famous list of the features of Manhattan
living that he also hates—busses with drivers yelling for people to
move to the rear and going up and down in elevators when you want
to go outside and having guys fitting your pants at Brooks Brothers.
(Taxicabs are substituted in the novel for a 72nd Street movie house
with fake clouds on the ceiling mentioned in the short story.) The list
stresses situations that jam one tightly in unnatural atmospheres with
other people and involve being touched—something that particularly
unnerves Holden and Salinger himself as indicated at the conclusion of
his interview with Betty Eppes.[11]

The important comment in the conversation, however, which is even
more highly italicized in the novel than in the short story, is Holden's
insistence that he *hates* school. The crucial difference between Holden

and Sally, whom he calls "queen of the phonies" and "a royal pain in the ass" (173; the *New Yorker* had cut the sentence short at "pain"), after unsuccessfully proposing to her, is that Sally's reaction to school—as indeed everything else—is the predictably fashionable one. It's OK to be "bored" with school (one does not want to be a "brain"); but to *hate* school, as Holden proclaims, is to make public unfashionably strong feelings, to reveal too much of one's self. It is not becoming to take something seriously enough to *hate* it. Sally is comfortably at home in the twilight world of J. Alfred Prufrock, measuring out her life "with coffee spoons," or of the typist in *The Waste Land,* who after casual sex with a man for whom she has no feeling, "smooths her hair with automatic hand, . . . and puts a record on the gramophone" (III. 255–56).

Although Holden, as critics have thronged to point out, shares much of the phoniness he complains of in others, he differs from those he meets in that he still has genuinely passionate feelings that have atrophied in what we would now call conformist clones. The overwhelming question that he poses for the many readers who have become absorbed in his fate is—can he survive in a clockwork-controlled world? The question is not, as it is in "I'm Crazy," can he hope to be successful, but can he survive at all? He realizes this as he is walking down Fifth Avenue and suddenly fears that he may never be able to get across a street. He calls to his dead brother Allie not to let him disappear; there is no one left in this world to whom he can turn. At this critical juncture, he decides never to go home or to another school again.

Holden as Catcher

To read many critiques of *The Catcher in the Rye,* especially those fabricated by ever-vigilant censors still trying to keep the novel out of classrooms and out of the hands, minds, and hearts of young people whose cloning the establishment has not yet completed, one would suppose that Holden remains, as we find him during the crisis just cited, "cynical, defiant, and blind." These adjectives have been provided by John Aldridge, a celebrated critic of the decline of post–World War II American character as exhibited in its popular literature.

In this first criticism of Salinger to be featured in a major academic study of contemporary American fiction, Aldridge is responsible for what has become a classic misreading of the novel. After observing that Holden's innocence is "a compound of urban intelligence, juvenile contempt, and *New Yorker* sentimentalism," Aldridge proceeds to inform readers that the boy "remains at the end what he was at the beginning," since the world of "phonies, bores, deceivers, and perverts," which he perceives is but "part of the truth which Holden does not see, and, as it turns out, is never able to see."[12]

The Catcher in the Rye is thus, as Aldridge perceives it, and as many others have since, including John Lennon's assassin Mark David Chapman,[13] a latter-day *Peter Pan* about a little boy who never grows up but continues to indulge his juvenile fantasies. The novel is regarded as a modern picaresque about a singularly inept rogue tilting with windmills that finally unseat his reason, so that he must be sent to rusticate near Disneyland. If Holden, however, cannot be said to be "cured" as the novel ends (assuming that there is something permanently wrong with him and that he has not just been passing through a phase), he does undergo a major transformation through the last twenty-five pages of the novel, particularly in chapter 25, which probably only coincidentally carries the same number as the Christmas Day that Holden earlier feels does not seem to be coming.

Pressed by little sister Phoebe, Holden discloses at the end of the twenty-second chapter the famous vision that gives the novel its title. It describes Holden's desire to be a "catcher in the rye," who would stand at the edge of "some crazy cliff" and keep the little kids who are running around the field without paying attention to where they are going from falling over the edge, thus allowing them forever to remain playing some carefree game. Before Phoebe puts his dream to the test, however, Holden must undergo a final, supremely disillusioning experience when he flees his home again in anticipation of spending a peaceful night with the best teacher he ever had, Mr. Antolini, with whom students could "kid around" without losing respect for him.

Abundant commentaries of the novel have taken the position that Antolini serves as a voice for the author and that the advice he gives Holden—to ponder psychoanalyst Wilhelm Stekel's injunction that "the mark of the immature man is that he wants to die nobly for a cause, while the mark of the mature man is that he wants to live humbly for one" (244)—may give Holden a sense of direction, and thus help him to avoid the horrible fall toward which Antolini feels he is heading. Such a position, however, seems entirely out of keeping with the whole tenor of Salinger's writing. Certainly Seymour Glass, who emerges as the true "poet-seer" in Salinger's book of saints, is no disciple of Stekel's, but we need not jump so far ahead to argue the point, since the applicability of Antolini's advice to Holden is confounded by *Catcher* itself.

In the first place, Antolini is shown, during Holden's actual crisis, to be quite as unreliable a savior as anyone else that Holden has encountered in the forbidding city. Although it is apparent that Holden is worn out and sleepy when he even commits the inexcusable gaffe of yawning in Antolini's face (247), Antolini, quite boozed up, insists on rambling on and on, chiding, questioning, and warning the boy when he should have let him get to sleep and have deferred such a session until Holden was rested up for it. Like everyone else, he has pushed the boy too far, too fast. (So, of course, has Salinger. In dealing with this much-analyzed episode, we must remember that a skilled author subordinates each part of the action to the design of the whole. Salinger must come up with an adequately convincing stratagem to get the exhausted Holden out of Antolini's apartment, so that he will not be rested up the next day when he must endure his supreme crisis.)

Thus he has Antolini commit the final mistake of patting the restlessly sleeping boy, who has exhibited throughout the novel an almost pathological sensitivity (seemingly shared by his creator) to being touched. This is enough to send Holden running from the house at the same time that it subsequently permits him to suffer further doubts about the ambiguities of human motivation. This issue is dealt with at great length in Holden's comments to Phoebe about whether the behavior of lawyers is altruistic or self-seeking. A point that needs to be remembered, however, is that the question about Antolini's sexual proclivities cannot be answered by the readers any more than by Holden, for the whole episode is not about Antolini's but about Holden's state of mind. Holden's final comment on the matter that maybe Antolini "just liked to pat guys on the head when they're asleep" (253) shows only that Holden is beginning to learn to distrust snap judgments and that he is unfamiliar with traditional beliefs about the possibly therapeutic effect of the laying on of hands.

The important reason for being skeptical about the value of Antolini's advice is not this episode at all, but that during the final pages of the novel he is proved wrong about the horrible consequences of Holden's fall. For the next morning the exhausted Holden does indeed experience a fall but with vastly different consequences from those Antolini feared.

After a restless night in Grand Central Station (an experience a solicitous Holden tells readers to avoid for it will depress them), he reaches the lowest point of his despair when he begins to feel he may disappear and calls out to his dead brother for help. He decides that after he runs away from the city, he will pose as a deaf-mute and hide his children, should he have any. He communicates his intentions to Phoebe in a note requesting a final meeting, which he leaves at the office of her school.

The following material has led to some of the most misguided and bigoted criticism in literary history. As Holden is walking up the stairs to the school to leave the note, he sees "fuck you" written on the wall and rubs it off with his hand. Then, as he is going down a different staircase, he sees the same words on the wall, but this time scratched in with a knife so that he cannot efface them. Finally even in the timeless peace of the Egyptian tomb room at the Metropolitan Museum of Art, he finds them again, written in red crayon under glass. This final depressing discovery leads to the most distressing epiphany of his quest, "You can't ever find a place that's nice and peaceful because there isn't any" (264).

In the passage leading to this bleak climactic perception, the obscenity that combines the grossest concept of sexual intercourse with the ugliest contempt for human dignity occurs six times, always in quotation marks. Although Holden is often scolded for swearing, he never uses the word "fuck" himself; rather he is driven into a violent rage by seeing it. His passionate feelings are exacerbated by finding the word where innocent children might see it, and he attributes the abomination to "some perverty bum." He tries to remove the offending words wherever he finds them (some cannot be effaced) and fantasizes himself catching the culprit and smashing "his head on the stone steps until he was good and goddam dead and bloody," though sadly he recognizes that he "wouldn't have the guts to do it" (261).

(Digression—Those Naughty Words)

Because the word "fuck" appears six times, *Catcher* has been countless times condemned as obscene by individuals or groups seeking to have it censored or removed from public schools or libraries. Rarely is there any evidence that the self-appointed guardians of virtue initiating these demands have read the entire novel to learn the context in which the word appears. The whole effort in itself only serves to confirm Holden's cheerless perception that people only notice what they wish; at the same time it provides a depressing example of people's not recognizing an ally when one appears. Instead of condemning the novelist for using profane language, those concerned should come to the defense of the quixotic hero who tries to rid the world of such outrages and their perpetrators. Salinger's intentions, however, have been as sadly misconstrued as Holden fears his own may be if he is found trying to remove them. Someone will suspect that he wrote them—someone who unctuously objects to them but does not trouble to remove them.

If the argument of the would-be censors is that innocent children would never come across such words if they did not see them in the novel, they are far more naive than Holden. Certainly they must not have looked around in public places.[14] When I started elementary school, some of the first reading matter I encountered on my trips to school was an even uglier version of the sentiment Holden despises, chalked on high board fences, inciting in a changing neighborhood where there were severe racial tensions, incest as well as fornication.

Generally before World War II such language was indicated by * * * * in published texts, and it was purged altogether—along with much milder sentiments—from the cinema by special interest groups who hoped to keep film as far as possible from life. (As I write, changing fashions in the flight from reality have moved to the other end of a spectrum. I lost count of the number of times the character played by Dennis Hopper says "fuck" in the film *Blue Velvet,* but he must have set a new record. I hope no one feels compelled to challenge it, for the point that this speaker was a nasty man could have been made with less distasteful monotony.) The publishers of Salinger's novel are to be complimented, however, for printing the words where they are essential to convey unmistakably the reactions of someone who *hates* them rather than merely acquiesces in prevailing community tastes.

The Fall and the Vision

Immediately after Holden makes the humiliating self-assessment that he lacks guts (earlier he acknowledges that he is "too yellow" not to join "a goddam secret fraternity" at Pencey Prep [217]), he has to take a purgative trip to the museum bathroom. As he is leaving, he "sort of" passes out and experiences a fall, as a result of which he says, he could have "killed himself," but "a funny thing" is that he lands on his side with little injury and afterwards "felt better" (265). He has found his cause, he has failed it, and he has fallen; but he has survived the experience, and he learns from it.

He begins to feel better just in time to cope with the most serious problem he has yet to face when Phoebe arrives for their appointment with her bag packed to challenge his ambition to play catcher in the rye and announces that she is going to accompany him on his journey. Holden realizes that he is not prepared to take her away from a secure home and argues, ironically, that she has to stay here to play the role of Benedict Arnold in the school Christmas pageant. He is frightened when she wishes to follow his example in refusing to go back to school, and she slips away when Holden attempts to take her hand. He sees that "she's a madman sometimes" (270), too; and he becomes depressed when she asks him to "please" keep her Christmas money for her.

He manages, however, to induce her to ride the carousel in the Central Park zoo. With almost too ponderous significance, the song it is playing, "very jazzy and funny," is Cole Porter's "Smoke Gets in Your Eyes" about the tearful effects of a failed vision. Phoebe joins the other kids in trying to grab for the gold rings (which are ironically only brass-plated iron—fit emblems of a society that washes a glittering surface over a shoddy foundation) that protrude from the end of an arm that extends out from beside the carousel just close enough to tempt the riders to risk grabbing for the prize. Holden is afraid that Phoebe may fall off the horse, as the kids he dreamed of protecting might fall off the cliff; but he has abandoned his vision of the night before (he does not have the guts to accept its consequences), and he displays now an acceptance—if never approval—of things as they are on "sort of a lousy Day" (270). He does not say anything to Phoebe, but he informs the reader, that he cannot do anything to stop her, because "the thing with kids is, if they want to grab for the gold ring, you have to let them do it and not say anything. If they fall off, they fall off, but it's bad if you say anything to them" (273–74).

So much for Antolini's rhetoric; so much for Holden's vision. He has abandoned his madman's dream of being a catcher in the rye and realized that you have to let kids grow up, take their own chances, and make their own mistakes. The very last sentence of this chapter, which narrates the destruction of his illusions, shows, however, that he has not lost his admiration of even a fleeting innocence. Phoebe, he tells the reader, just looks "so damn *nice*" whirling around in aimless circles grabbing for the elusive gold ring that he wishes "you could've been there" (275).

What of Holden beyond this moment? As he tells us in the brief final chapter, "How do you know what you're going to do till you *do* it?" (276). In what Holden has earlier called his favorite novel, *The Great Gatsby,* Daisy Buchanan asks, "What do people plan?" Holden does not know the answer any more than she does—he is not the planning type. Salinger leaves the question of whether Holden will "apply himself" up in the air and never returns to follow the character beyond the end of his boyhood. One gets the feeling, however, that despite the difference between this Holden and the earlier version of the character in "I'm Crazy," he, too, "wasn't going to be one of those successful guys," but one also gets the feeling that he is not going to let himself get as worked up again about his future as he has during the days of lonely wandering and questioning described in the novel. As he does take Phoebe home again, one gets the deflating feeling that the world does not amount to much but one has to put up with it as it is. This conclusion, however, is Holden's, not that of the author, who leaves Holden behind in his quest for Seymour Glass.

Salinger returned to a Holden Caulfield-like character only once more in what has been the least understood of his *Nine Stories*, "De Daumier-Smith's Blue Period." Holden would certainly agree with De Daumier-Smith's final gesture of leaving everyone to their own devices, but he would not grasp the meaning of the cryptic "everybody is a nun" as a more elegant and spiritual paraphrase of his own final reflections about "missing everybody." Holden remains an entirely earthy sensory character; there is nothing mystical about his vision. Salinger was headed, however, for other realms—as T. S. Eliot had been after "The Hollow Men"; but like Eliot, he was also never to attract quite so many followers as he had with his earthbound quester. That Holden's quest, however, leads him not out of this world, but right back into it, is one matter that must be considered in assessing reasons for *The Catcher in the Rye*'s extraordinary reputation.

Deinitiation

If one is determined to plunge madly ahead and apply terminology to a work whose creator and protagonist both distrust logical analysis, *The Catcher in the Rye* can probably best be pigeonholed not as a picaresque tale of the dark journey (although Holden sees little light during his wanderings—he spends much of the one full day reported in the darkness of the Empire Theatre and Radio City Music Hall), but as a bildungsroman, that term difficult to render into English for a tale of education or growth or perhaps most nearly enlightenment. An even more useful approach, however, may be to consider the novel as a culmination of a long American tradition of the ancient ritual of initiation, as Peter Freese does in his dissertation *Die Initiationreise* (The journey of initiation: The adolescent hero in the modern american novel, with a special study of J. D. Salinger's *The Catcher in the Rye*; University of Kiel, 1971). This study serves to suggest the universality of the story as perceived by a European scholar who has shown a much deeper sensitivity to the archetypal elements underlying the novel than most American commentators. Americans have been so entranced by Salinger's control of a Manhattan adolescent's idiom and weltanschauung (to appropriate yet another untranslatable term) that they have often not looked beneath its authentically realistic surface for underlying universal patterns.

Freese begins with analyses of sixty American novels from Charles Brockden Brown's *Arthur Mervyn* to Norman Mailer's *Why Are We in Vietnam?* and of some hundred critical statements on the concept of "initiation" in literary criticism. He then presents a catalog of ten elements present in all concepts of the journey of initiation, seeing it as "a process of conversion and development consisting of three phases: exit, transition, re-entrance," which "results in such a fundamental change that it is imagined as the death of the old and the birth of a new person." The study concludes with a section on Salinger's novel, showing that it contains "all ten of the constituents found to be present in the process of initiation" and presents the thesis that the concept of this process "enables the critic to see a new coherence in the seemingly unconnected episodes of Holden's odyssey."[15]

Freese's argument not only places this controversial novel of adolescence in a tradition that extends back to the preliterate past, but also has particular importance for "new world" fiction by providing an impressive means of appreciating the novel as not only a realistic, but a ritualistic work. The caution that one must always bear in mind in working with such an approach is that the author may not, like John Steinbeck in *The Red Pony,* also have had such resonances specifically in mind. As we shall see, however, in the subsequent discussion of Salinger's *Nine Stories,* an author's intuitions may carry him far beyond what he intended. The imagination that perceives archetypal patterns in human experience may influence an author to structure the narrative in a way that he or she does not immediately understand to impose communicable form upon the chaos of experience. As William Faulkner, who admired Salinger's novel, wrote to Malcolm Cowley, "Art is simpler than people think because there is so little to write about. All the moving things are eternal in man's history and have been written before, and if a man writes hard enough, sincerely enough, humbly enough and with unalterable determination never, never to be quite satisfied with it, he will repeat them."[16]

Salinger had indeed penetrated into the flux of daily disorder to discover patterns "eternal in man's history," and this achievement alone might adequately explain the extraordinary reception of his novel; but before proceeding from its identification with the initiation story to the question of the reasons for its particular success, we must recognize that in *Catcher,* as Freese points out, Holden does not have the tutor "to help and counsel him" that the hero usually does. Holden's story is not the familiar one (as in Mozart's *The Magic Flute*) of the initiation of a newcomer through an established ritual performed by experienced elders, but the account of an idealistic youth receiving through bored and self-seeking counselors a grim introduction into the fragmentation of American life. (An example of the more traditional tutor-student pattern in a contemporary work is John Barth's allegorical fantasy, *Giles Goat-Boy,* 1966.)

All sorts of initiation rites are a daily feature of American life. Especially for members of the affluent upper middle class from which Salinger and Holden come, membership is available upon acceptance into the social fraternities at Ivy League colleges, most residential institutions, and even the private prep schools. These groups bind the chosen few into brotherhoods for life through closely guarded rituals that are usually debased versions of the traditional rites of the various Masonic orders, themselves often under fire for their exclusivity and political influence. For more boisterous fraternizing, there are the Elks, Moose, Red Men, Golden Eagles, and others that have vanished since their heyday in the Gilded Age. There are even, as Holden protests to an uncomprehending Sally Hayes at the adolescent boarding schools, "dirty little goddam cliques" of basketball players, Catholics, intellectuals, bridge-players, even subscribers to the Book-of-the-Month Club (170), as well as the more ominous imitations of the college brotherhoods, one of which Holden is "too yellow not to join." Not all these loosely structured groups have specific rituals, but a surprising number (like my own high school newspaper) do.

Americans are great joiners, but this craving for belonging is not satisfied by any national institution, such as has often been provided in Western European nations by a rigorous class structure or compulsory military training, which, though often undesirable in themselves, provide a basis for internal order and the formation of a clearly defined opposition party. The proliferation in American society of small, exclusive societies, often only minimally different from one another but violently at odds over trivial issues, produces a fragmented culture in which pressure groups contend for the support of the naive and inexperienced on the basis of uninformed prejudices, so that people like Holden end up "missing everybody," without any standards for making disinterested judgments. Holden's "initiation" has led only to the confirmation of his early reflection, when his history teacher observes that "life *is* a game that one plays according to the rules," that "if you get on the side where all the hot-shots are, then it's a game. . . . But if you get on the *other* side . . . then what's a game about it?" (12). He has never wanted to join the winning side, but he has hoped that he might keep kids from getting hooked on the game; when, however, he sees the kids on the carousel, whirling around with the crowd, but each preoccupied with grabbing the phony rings, he has realized that you cannot save people from themselves. (This is the point that Mark David Chapman and others have missed.)

His self-imposed quest has led him to an acceptance of the world as it is, but it is a grudging acceptance that certainly gives no promise that he will become a team player. His "initiation" is actually a deinitiation that confirms his dissociation from a world that he has come to understand better. He has not abandoned his defiance, however; he is still a "hater," but he is no longer blinded by his own romantic vision—he has cleared the smoke from his eyes. As he is a great "hater," so also is he a "lover," missing all the still deluded fellow beings who finally find form in Salinger's "Zooey" as the Fat Lady, for whom he feels a compassionate affection.

The Popularity of *The Catcher in the Rye*

Since, as Freese observed in 1971, juvenile protagonists have been used often in American fiction to convey the loneliness and confusion of modern life, what has given Salinger's novel its particular staying power? In concurring in the decision to make *Catcher* the midsummer selection of the Book-of-the-Month Club in 1951, the distinguished jury, including popular novelists John P. Marquand and Christopher Morley, observed that while the novel recalled "the comedies and tragedies of Booth Tarkington's *Seventeen*," the 1917 novel that had been for the preceding thirty-four years most widely appreciated as the classic portrayal of American adolescence, it "reaches far deeper into reality," so that, "to anyone who has ever brought up a son, every page of Mr. Salinger's novel would be a source of wonder and delight—and concern."[17] The brief statement, however, left these flattering generalities unexamined.

Early American reviews of the novel, written as often by competitors seeking to outshine the author, were no more prophetically accurate than are most later American reviews written under the pressure of short deadlines.[18] The most perceptive early review came from abroad, contributed to London's traditional popular weekly, *Punch,* by R. G. G. Price, who found that "the weakness of the novel is its sentimentality," which he suspected was "in character, that the author has not invented it but approves of it." Price concludes that this may "be merely the reaction of a corrupt European, who prefers a soft surface and hard core."[19] Price is certainly correct about the sentimentality of the novel, which many subsequent commentators have observed, but what may be its weakness from a "stiff-upper-lip" English point of view is likely to have been one of its principal appeals to American adolescents, who shared Holden's sense of being "deinitiated" from a society in which sensitive persons felt alienated. Price was quite right, however, in alerting British readers what to expect from this overseas visitor.

The sentimentality that Price distrusts in the author is the Rousseauesque belief in the virtues of a primal state of innocence before the corrupting rise of civilized institutions, reinforced by the biblical concept of the Garden of Eden and the superior vision of innocent childhood that colors Wordsworth's "Immortality Ode," one of the highwater marks of British romanticism that is probably more cherished in America. The English, in fact, passed through their period of enthusiasm for this vision in the eighteenth century when the riches of the New World fueled the blooming of an Adamic garden world (I refer to the British architect Robert Adam, not the biblical patriarch). The dehumanizing features of the industrial revolution, following the political revolutions in America and France, disillusioned the English about any fundamental goodness in people (the Welsh and Irish have not participated to the same extent in this devolution) and led them to place a premium upon a well-managed administration of tough policies.

Americans, however, cherishing George Washington's warning against entanglements with the Old World as the supreme piece of native wisdom and despising any hereditary aristocracy, continued to place trust in the natural aristocracy of the self-made individual, whose genius had manifested itself free of the influence of any restraining institutions. This predisposition was fostered by the continuing utter irrelevancy to the nature and needs of American society of the kind of preparatory schools that Salinger and Holden Caulfield attended.

Efforts were made, of course, especially under pressure from condescending foreign visitors like Mrs. Frances Trollope and Charles Dickens, to teach people manners once they had made money, and the production of etiquette books like Thomas E. Hill's *Manual of Social and Business Forms* (first published, Chicago, 1873) became the new bibles of vulgarians "learning how to behave," as Arthur Schlesinger, Sr., titled a history of the genre. This movement, however, often resulted in such excesses of propriety that even William Dean Howells, who had successfully overcome a frontier background to become the inheritor of Boston's literary establishment by spending the Civil War years being seasoned in Venice, was moved to express doubts about the virtues of the establishment in his novel *The Rise of Silas Lapham,* the most perceptive fictional portrayal of the Gilded Age nouveaux riches: "It is certain that our manners and customs go for more in life than our qualities. The price that we pay for civilization is the fine yet impassable differentiation of these. Perhaps we pay too much, but it will not be possible to persuade those who have the difference in their favor that this is so."[20]

Howells's friend Henry James, taking the side of manners, removed permanently to England (his female Holden Caulfield, Daisy Miller, came to a regrettable end); but America's twentieth-century novels, culminating in the book that became Salinger's Buddy Glass's *Tom Sawyer,* Fitzgerald's *The Great Gatsby,* apotheosized as "worth the whole damn bunch" the figure of the self-made idealist who "sprang from his Platonic conception of himself," despite his garish taste and dubious morals.

What Price's review in *Punch* suggests can be appreciated by reversing his terms to describe an "innocent American preference for a tough-guy surface and a soft core," the kind of personality exemplified by Gatsby, who collaborated with the man who fixed the 1919 World Series in order to finance a doomed grail quest. Indeed in the statement about the Book-of-the-Month Club's selection of *Catcher,* Clifton Fadiman, long the *New Yorker's* principal book reviewer, observed in passing that "Holden's relationship with Phoebe is the tender heart of a story that is only superficially hardboiled"; but Fadiman had simply taken for granted that American audiences would prove susceptible to a character whose prickly surface conceals a heart of gold.[21]

Bad form has always been more objectionable to the English than foppish style, for they have been disinclined to believe that loutishness disguises a noble interior, whereas unaffected Americans suspect that good manners mask a confidence man (as in circles attempting to become fashionable they often did). The Dickensian stereotype of the "self-made man" is Josiah Bounderby in *Hard Times*, whose name alone conveys the novelist's attitude toward this bigoted hypocrite. D. H. Lawrence began to challenge this traditional view, but ended up by reversing Henry James's route and going to the States.

Generally, however, from Samuel Richardson's *Pamela* to recent films like Stephen Frears's *My Beautiful Laundrette*, a well-mannered determination to take one's proper place in society, even if guile must be used, has been preferred to the crude spontaneity of those who cannot or will not play the game (one of Holden Caulfield's closest counterparts in English fiction is perhaps Morgan, as played by David Warner in the 1966 film thus titled, who ends up tending the flower beds in a nice and peaceful asylum). The English preference appears to be for quests that, however arduous the route, end in triumph, whereas Americans, in contradiction of myths about the dream, cultivate fables that end in at least material defeat and usually disaster. Holden avoids the fall that the irredeemably romantic Antolini (who has apparently married enough money not to be subject to too much pressure from reality) foresees, but he ends up disillusioned and alienated, recognizing the game but reluctant to join it.

Efforts, however, to isolate the particular reasons for the continuing popularity of *Catcher* have not proved enlightening. A great many books about Salinger have been announced, but few have appeared, because, I suspect, once enthusiasts began to inspect the work closely they became depressed by what they found to say about it. An intriguing field remains open.

Most attempts to account for the novel's reputation go no further than a statement published somewhere in England, compiled most likely in 1963 by the staff of the library of the United States Information Service in response to someone's request for its list of a dozen best American postwar novels. This somewhat idiosyncratic list contains, besides *Catcher*, James Baldwin's *Another Country*, Saul Bellow's *Adventures of Augie March*, Truman Capote's *The Grass Harp*, John Cheever's *The Wapshot Chronicle*, Joseph Heller's *Catch-22*, Jack Ker-

ouac's *On the Road*, Norman Mailer's *Naked and the Dead*, Bernard Malamud's *New Life*, Philip Roth's *Letting Go*, William Styron's *Lie Down
in Darkness*, and John Updike's *Poorhouse Fair*. It reports of *Catcher* that
"it soon became first favourite among students in the Western world
and its translation into a dozen or more languages has now placed it
high on the list in Eastern countries as well." It describes Holden as
"an American schoolboy who, in the bitterness of failure and being
dropped by his school, plays 'hookey' for three days and nights in New
York" and explains that "his predicament touches a chord in the heart
of all schoolboys and there is a peculiar fascination in the way Salinger
has caught the sound of his speech."[22] "Playing 'hookey,'" leaves the
impression that Holden is just another naughty boy carrying on the
tradition of Thomas Bailey Aldrich's *Story of a Bad Boy* (1870) and
Booth Tarkington's *Penrod* (1914), who will soon see the error of his
ways and be back in the fold, perhaps working for USIS. The remarks
might have introduced a *Reader's Digest* condensation of *Catcher* if one
had ever been contemplated and Salinger had permitted it. Anyone led
to read the novel by this introduction might have been in for a shock.

The Rosen Report

Gerald Rosen gets much closer to dealing adequately with the phe-
nomenon of *Catcher* in a 1977 special issue of *American Quarterly*, that
reassessed twentieth-century documents. Editor Bruce Kulick did not
include in the issue (unlike customary procedures) an introduction explaining who had selected and analyzed the documents and what principles had guided their choices. The selection is, however, an
impressive one, as the documents chosen (see enumeration above, p.
6) deal with important aspects of change in American culture.

Rosen reaches the striking conclusion about *Catcher* that "what we
have here in miniature, in 1951, is the prescient portrait of an attempt
to create a counterculture."[23] A problem with Rosen's thesis, however,
is that Salinger's novel has outlasted the counterculture it presaged, so
that seeing the author as a John the Baptist for the Beats or Hippies
(for whom he had no use) only emphasizes the failure of the counterculture examined by Theodore Roszak to sustain itself.[24] Rosen is not
principally concerned with politicized countercultures, however, so
much as with Salinger's early involvement in the importation of Asian
religious doctrines, later accelerated, guiding principles in the formation of an American life-style. Even the enthusiasm for these, which

reached a peak with the successes in the late 1960s and early 1970s of the transcendental meditation movement under the guidance of Maharishi Mahesh Yogi (with which Salinger is not known to have had any connection), has since declined in popularity in the United States to the point that they serve as only a passing phase of the quest for tranquility in Woody Allen's *Hannah and Her Sisters* (1986). In concentrating on the importance of Eastern thought in Salinger's work, Rosen fails to get at the continuing significance of Holden Caulfield's relationship to the mainstream of American life, since the oriental influences on Salinger are much more strongly evidenced in the later and less enduringly popular Glass family stories.

Rosen makes a much more promising start when he observes that "the radical nature of Salinger's portrayal of disappointment with American society, so much like Twain's in *Huck Finn,* was probably as much of the reason that *Catcher* (like *Huck*) was banned from schools and colleges as were the few curse words around which the battle was publicly fought" (548); but he abandons further tunneling into the American psyche because he is bent on guru hunting.

While recognizing that Antolini is "blind to the existential reality of Holden's condition," Rosen approves some of his advice, but argues that what Holden needs even more is "a living adult" as a model (561), not recognizing that if there were such an adult, there would be no novel, at least certainly not this novel. Although Rosen warns in his conclusion that readers "must be careful not to ask Salinger or anyone else to provide us with [an] illusory 'Answer'" (562), he still tends to see Holden as much like the quite different and even more hopelessly situated fifteen-year-old who is the title character of James Purdy's *Malcolm* (1959). Malcolm announces soon after his abandonment by his father, "I suppose if somebody would tell me what to do, I would do it," and he is predictably driven to death at an early age by exploitative advisors.[25] Holden, however, is a poor listener throughout the novel.

Rosen also fails to see the importance of his correction of a common misconception about the novel, which he relegates to a footnote (557), explaining that Holden could hardly be telling his story to a therapist at a California sanitarium. Rosen could use far stronger evidence than he does to make his point, and his speculation that at one point "Holden seems to be addressing *the reader*" is unnecessarily cautious. Holden *is* addressing the reader throughout the novel, from an opening statement "the first thing you'll probably want to know is where I was born" (information a therapist would already have)—to his final—

"Don't ever tell anybody anything" (a curious comment if addressed to a therapist).

Holden is appealing directly to a reader he hopes is going to be interested in listening to him. As the instructional tone of the very last words, "you start missing everybody," indicates, Holden does not need a guide or role model; he *is* the guide, as is especially apparent from such bits of gratuitous advice as not to sleep on the benches at Grand Central Station, "It'll depress you" (242). Rosen, like many other commentators, overlooks the colossal arrogance with which Salinger has endowed Holden, who may seek help from other people, but never advice. Are young readers throughout the world predisposed to pay attention to such an authority among their peers? Apparently. The question is really just what has attracted them so much to his message.

The Ohmann/Miller Correspondence

The loftiest debate over Salinger's novel was not, however, conducted by a peer group forum of a kind Seymour Glass might have instigated, but waged in 1976 and 1977 between two editors of *College English*, an official organ of the National Council of Teachers of English, in *Critical Inquiry*, one of the United States's most prestigious humanities forums, published at the University of Chicago.

The opening volley of what was apparently not originally intended as an exchange was fired by the more recent editor, Richard Ohmann, in collaboration with his wife Carol. Observing that since Bantam Books had taken over the paperbound edition of *The Catcher in the Rye* in April 1964, it had sold probably 10 million copies, the Ohmanns proposed in "Reviewers, Critics, and *The Catcher in the Rye*" to investigate how the novel became a classic, announcing frankly in their opening statement that the essay was "a case study of capitalist criticism" to determine "what reviewers and what academic critics after them did see in the novel and what they might have seen in it."[26] The Ohmanns were at the time widely known and respected as principal advocates and practitioners of Marxist literary criticism, and it quickly became clear that they were not conducting just another objective survey of past criticism of the novel.

Arguing that reviewers "assumed that a novel's most important function is mimetic and that insofar as it succeeds as representation, it succeeds as fiction" (19), the Ohmanns believed that in blaming Holden's predicament on himself and some spiritual illness, these reviewers "tend away from precise description of the society Salinger renders in *Catcher*" (25). They maintain that the phoniness Holden deplores is rather "rooted in the economic and social arrangements of capitalism and in their concealment" (27), a statement supported by Holden's disgruntled aside to the reader after being told by his history teacher that "life *is* a game that one plays according to the rules," and that "if you get on the side where all the hot-shots are, then it's a game all right" (12). When, however, the Ohmanns go on to observe that faced by the evil world of a dehumanized society, one has only three options, which prove to be much like those that William Faulkner also proposed—to "do the best you can with the society, work for a better one, or flee society altogether"[27]—they conclude that "only the second answer responds to the critical feeling that dominates the book" (33).

The basis for this unsupported assertion is hard to fathom, although it proves the key to the Ohmanns' reading of the novel. Nowhere in the book is there any evidence that Holden has thoughts of working for a better world. His vision of functioning as a catcher in the rye reflects a subsequently abandoned desire to keep the innocent sequestered from society altogether. When at the end of the novel, he sees the futility of this hope and observes that if kids grabbing for a gold ring fall off, they fall off, but you should not say anything, it is another flight from social commitment. The only initiative that Holden takes in the novel is his unsuccessful campaign to erase all the dirty words he spots, but this, too, is an effort to maintain a hothouse innocence. The Ohmanns, like many others, apparently sympathize with Antolini's borrowed precept about working humbly for a cause, but Holden shows no signs of accepting this advice, which would require perseverance rather than temperamental outbursts.

The problem with the Ohmanns' argument is that they are not just reporting a clinical study of the reception of the novel; they like the book and are trying to find some way to approve. But if they followed strictly their own anticapitalist structures, they would have to reject such entropic defeatism as subversive.

This is exactly what an orthodox Russian Marxist critic has done. Writing "On J. D. Salinger's Novel" for *Inostrannaia literatur* (Foreign literature) in 1960, Vera Panova asks, "Why should the confused wanderings of an ill-fated, infantile Holden Caulfield concern us?" and answers, "He is a rich man's kid, a loafer, and it would not seem that the reader has any reason to worry about him."[28] Panova confuses fiction with document when she goes on to hope that "when the chaos of confusion" in Holden abates, "*may* he find that elevated goal, the one in the name of which one wants to live and for the sake of which it is not frightening to die" (italics mine). The possible pursuit of such a goal, however, is something not foreshadowed by the novel; Holden is, in fact, not "confused" at the end of his story—he is tired of hearing cant about applying one's self and ready to take things as they come.

While the Ohmanns' conclusion that American criticism of the novel has been capitalist-oriented is accurate, it is hardly surprising, and it does not explain why the novel has sold millions of copies when some of this criticism has been negative and other novels more praised when approached from the same critical viewpoint have not fared as well. Their further theory that the disapproving critics' view that "to reject [American] society is to reject society itself" is a false equation seems an unarguable assessment of parochial bias, but it tells us nothing about Holden's problems about loss of innocence, a concern that far antedates capitalism. Holden's likes and dislikes cannot be firmly affixed to any one economic or political revelation; his view is most nearly that of the character in Jean-Paul Sartre's play *No Exit,* who announces, "Hell is other people." As for Holden's creator, he has disassociated himself from any society as far as is practically possible. One gets the feeling that the Ohmanns simply cannot adjust themselves to Holden's not so much hating growing up in a capitalist world as hating growing up at all. Their theories would apply very well to the earlier conception of Holden as presented in the short story, "I'm Crazy," where he did see himself as a victim of the system. At the end of *Catcher,* however, Holden places himself above any systems. It is hard for many real people, as well as the fictional Sally Hayes, to realize what a great "hater" Holden is and how much Holden's intensity may have been admired by generations of readers who cannot hope to match his example. At the end of *Catcher,* Holden is indeed condescendingly rejecting any society. The Ohmanns are even less willing than the critics they castigate to realize that he is dismissing their ideal as well.

Unfortunately, James E. Miller, Jr., who earlier had written probably the best appreciation of Salinger's work that has yet appeared, coming to the defense of a novel he thought entitled its author to "perhaps the pre-eminent position" in post–World War II American fiction, failed to perceive the shaky assumptions shaping the Ohmanns' reading and attacked them on purely partisan grounds. His stressing that "the Marxist critic is committed to persuading others that Marxism is the truest knowledge of ourselves and history" has nothing to do with the Ohmanns' article, since they do not provide a Marxist reading of the novel, though it might have served to answer Vera Panova. Because Miller failed to see that the article was the Ohmanns' attempt to rationalize their own sentimentality, he allowed the debate to degenerate into name-calling.

So much for American criticism at the summit. In their brief rejoinder, the Ohmanns rise to Miller's bait, so that the experience of reading the novel is shunted aside as the correspondence, like many before it, turns into an acrimonious exchange on the merits of political philosophies that are not shown to have much to do with the reception of this novel. A Marxist position on *Catcher* had, in fact, long before been articulated in Barbara Giles's essay "The Lonely War of J. D. Salinger" (*Mainstream,* February 1959)—ignored in the *Critical Inquiry* debate as generally elsewhere—which had taken the author, not his reviewers, to task for avoiding any discussion of real social problems.

Holden in the Lonely Crowd

Possible insights into the novel may be gained by turning from the sermons of literary critics to popular sociological speculations about the world that Salinger's novel mirrors.

A much consulted guide to the changing American character during the years of confusion when *Catcher* was published was *The Lonely Crowd* (1950), by David Riesman and Reuel Denney, social scientists at the University of Chicago, and Nathan Glazer, an associate editor of the American Jewish Forum's magazine *Commentary.* Holden Caulfield, however, could not be pigeonholed in any of the three principal categories of personalities explored in the book—tradition-directed (generally passive conformists to established rituals), inner-directed (able to function effectively in society without strict outside controls), and other-directed (controlled by contemporaries, personal friends, or mass media).

In fact, one of the few grounds on which many admirers and detractors of the book can meet is that Holden belongs not to any of the three types, but may be most satisfactorily described as "anomic," which the authors of *The Lonely Crowd* use to mean "ruleless," "ungoverned," "virtually synonymous with maladjusted" (238).[29] A disconcerting problem central to an understanding of the novel arises, however, with the recognition that Holden does not display "the lack of emotion and emptiness of expression" characteristic of "the ambu-

latory patients in the ward of modern culture," like Seymour Glass and
Teddy McArdle, but rather the "hysteria or outlawry . . . characteristic
of anomics in the societies depending on earlier forms of direction"
(281), as demonstrated by his vehement hatred of institutional confines
and his desire to take to the woods in emulation of the mountain men
who lived beyond the frontier in early America.

Holden displays remarkable success in resisting the "other-direc-
tion" of his "contemporaries," who are the undoing of James Purdy's
Malcolm; and, in fact, many readers may admire the novel because
Holden is an outsider rather then just another clone. Holden's problems stem from an inner-directed resistance to the regulations of an
influential segment of American society whose "keeping-up-with-the-
Joneses" life-style has already fossilized into a debilitating tradition.
Holden is the victim of the situation that H. L. Mencken characterized
with cynical aptness when he described the United States as the only
nation that had passed from barbarism to decadence without an intervening flowering of civilization. Holden yearns for the rejuvenating
rigors of barbarism while trapped in a reductivist Manhattan society,
which has changed only for the worse since Salinger captured its image.

Holden's situation is like that of Ike McCaslin in William Faulkner's
"The Bear," when he seeks to reject his heritage of proprietorship to
be "initiated" into an earlier culture that allowed people to live closer
to nature. (Faulkner, of course, sadly observed that this world was
gradually being destroyed by urbanized society, a sentiment that helps
account for his sympathy with Salinger's hero, who finds that the human race has disappeared.)

Holden's "deinitiation" is not, however, followed like Ike's by the
initiation he seeks, for Holden does not have an experienced tutor like
Sam Fathers to direct his induction into his chosen totem. Holden is
left entirely to his own devices with no perceptive or experienced adult
guidance. Phoebe does wonders for Holden's sagging morale, but she
proves more of a handicap than a help to his escape plans by showing
him that he is not yet ready to take responsibility for his dreams and
that he must move cautiously toward a life-style that may be suited
only to himself. She also implies that one must choose for one's self at
the age of the traditional initiation into a clan. Holden's hope that
Phoebe may still be able to make it in a world that he feels he must
reject is indicated by his comment that, when she pleads to run away
with him, he hates her most "because she wouldn't be in [her school's]
play any more if she went away with me" (268). He simply will not

make any compromises; and the only one that he does make at the very end is an agreement with himself not to try to recruit others to his views but to leave them to their own devices. The problem that remains at the end of the book is to what Holden may apply himself: will he indeed have the guts to conduct his isolated vigilante campaign against the "perverty bums" that deface the museums?

What Rosen and James Miller, along with many other critics, have failed to recognize is that Holden does have a vigilante viewpoint—something far from uncommon in the United States. It is somewhat unnerving, in fact, to be scrutinizing his behavior at the time of the tumult over Bernard Goetz, the New Yorker acquitted of shooting four youths who he claimed had harassed him on the subway. *The Catcher in the Rye* remains after three decades a contemporary work because the forces that agitated Holden Caulfield are still active and growing. He could have been tempted to react in the same way as Goetz, if he had the guts (remember his wishing to smash "the perverty bum's" head "on the stone steps" [217]). Lacking these, however, he would most likely have withdrawn angrily into the impotence he exhibits in a most literal form in his encounter with the prostitute.

What the Ohmanns, on the other hand, fail to recognize is that Holden is not looking forward to a better world, but backward to a world that primitivists fancy offered greater freedom to the individual. He seeks not a Marxist society, but a Rousseauesque world. If he is headed anywhere at the time the novel ends, it is not toward a collectivized society, but toward the kind of fragmented "commune" society of small isolated clans with which the hippies experimented. (Much diminished activity of this kind, in fact, still continues in some remote parts of the United States, while a more highly publicized but tiny group still persists in England.[30])

The Culture of Narcissism

The other-directed urban society that Holden seeks to flee is described in the following passage: "a way of life that is dying—the culture of competitive individualism, which in its decadence has carried the logic of individualism to the extreme of a war of all against all, the pursuit of happiness to the dead end of a narcissistic preoccupation with the self."[31] This comes not from one of Salinger's works nor one of the multitude of appraisals of *Catcher*, but from Christopher Lasch's prefatory description of his *Culture of Narcissism* (1979). Lasch provides

what proves a most accurate if unintentional description of Holden—
"the new narcissist is haunted not by guilt but by anxiety. He seeks
not to inflict his own certainties on others but to find a meaning in
life. Liberated from the superstitions of the past, he doubts even the
reality of his own existence. . . . Fiercely competitive in his demand
for approval and acclaim, he distrusts competition because he associates
it with an unbridled urge to destroy. . . . [He] demands immediate
gratification and lives in a state of restless, perpetually unsatisfied desire. . . . [He] has no interest in the future because, in part, he has so
little interest in the past" (22–23). Holden departs somewhat from
Lasch's description because he lacks a permissive attitude toward sex
and a desire for the favors of a paternalistic state, but these traits of
lazy adults could change if his adolescent passion is overwhelmed by
an undiscriminating acceptance of things as they are. Holden particularly exemplifies what Lasch regards as the "most telling proof" of the
"bankruptcy" of narcissistic culture, "indifference to the past," which
Holden denounces in his opening statement about "all that David Copperfield kind of crap" and in his conversation with his history teacher.
While this attitude seems superficially "cheerful and forward-looking,"
Lasch feels it derives from an "impoverishment of the psyche" that
makes people unable to ground their needs "in the experience of sat-
isfaction and contentment" (25). Holden never experiences contentment, except when he is in the company of children who will grow
up, or listening to records that can be broken, or watching a carousel
that is going to stop.

Lasch's book was written a quarter century after *Catcher,* but the
society it describes had already been developing three decades before
that when T. S. Eliot was reflecting his personal discontents in *The
Waste Land* and depicted his narrator shoring up fragments of the past
against his ruin. With the prescience of the clairvoyant artist, Salinger
was limning the fictional landscape, which the more pedestrian psy-
chosocial critic would later locate in reality. A potent reason to suppose
that *The Catcher in the Rye* has been read and reread many times by
several generations coming of age with continued enthusiasm is that
Holden Caulfield articulates the feelings that these readers have about
their decaying milieu, but cannot put into words—"What oft was
thought, but ne'er so well expressed," as poet Alexander Pope wrote
in the eighteenth century, still a valuable rule for distinguishing lasting literature from that which will be gone with the wind.

Salinger thus functioning not only as the voice of a particular gen-

eration (like Scott Fitzgerald), but also as the voice of passing generations at perhaps the most crucial point in their lives, during their
initiation into maturity, is what is responsible for his singular reputation. It is probably also the reason for the distraught reactions of those
who have sought to keep his novel out of schoolchildren's hands. It
takes an unaccustomed tough-mindeness to stare unblinkingly at the
world *Catcher* mirrors if, as Christopher Lasch argues, we have reached
the cultural crisis of a despairing society that "cannot face the future."

Lasch, ultimately and not surprisingly, turns to the vigilantism Holden dreamed of. Placing the blame for the sorry state of society principally on bureaucracy, Lasch rejects the argument that "common
sense" will at last prevail, arguing that it is not enough. In order to
break existing patterns of dependence, citizens will have to take solu-
tions of problems into "their own hands" (396).

As for Salinger, exercising the artist's prerogative of escaping into
art, after *Catcher* he abandoned the ways of the Wild West for Eastern
mysticism. He returned to a character who resembles Holden only once
again in what has proved the least appreciated of his *Nine Stories*, "De
Daumier-Smith's Blue Period." Holden would certainly appreciate the
climactic gesture of the young artist in this story when he stops teaching because he decides his students must choose their own fates; the
pseudonymous young man's cryptic comment that "Everybody is a
nun" is an elegant paraphrase of Holden's farewell observation about
"missing everybody." Thus some implications may be read back from
this story into a contemplation of Holden's future. The final vignette
in the short story portrays the narrator "investigating that most interesting of all summer-active animals, the American Girl in Shorts,"
something that the Holden of "I'm Crazy" would certainly have enjoyed. "Jean de Daumier-Smith," however, is far more sophisticated
and mystically minded than Holden and has not had his trouble with
schools, so he seems rather a transitional figure between Holden and
the Glass siblings rather than an older version of the disillusioned
catcher.

Salinger returned to Lasch's culture of narcissism also only once
again after *Catcher* in the story in *Nine Stories* that preceded "De Daumier-Smith's Blue Period," "Pretty Mouth and Green My Eyes." In
this he depicted for the first time since his early "Go See Eddie" the
adulterated and adulterous world of those who play the game in Manhattan. Since Salinger clearly despised this world, he abandoned it after
finding nothing new to report. He concluded his collection with

"Teddy," a study of one of the God seekers that he would pursue through the remaining stories attributed to Buddy Glass until he stopped publishing them. This is distinctly another story than Holden Caulfield's. We must leave him in sunny Southern California, waiting, with a host of others, for the earthquake promised in the region's apocalyptic literature that will send it sliding into the sea.

Chapter Four
A Nine-Story Cycle

J. D. Salinger has allowed to be collected only nine of the thirty short stories he is known to have published before the Glass family chronicle. Most disinterested editors would go along with this decision. Most of these stories have been either superseded by *The Catcher in the Rye* or may otherwise be regarded as apprentice works of a writer seeking to find the forms and content that satisfy him. He was not apparently satisfied with the results until he wrote "A Perfect Day for Bananafish," which began his almost exclusive association with the *New Yorker*, which lasted from 1948 to 1965, when his last short story appeared there.

Following the success of *The Catcher in the Rye* in 1951, Salinger did authorize the collection in 1953 of nine stories that he had published over the preceding five years, all but two in the *New Yorker*. These are not, however, just nine stories reprinted in what happened to be the order of their periodical publication. When one reads through the stories in their order in the American edition,[1] one develops a sense of an interconnectedness among them, of a progression that promotes the feeling that they constitute jointly an example of what Forrest Ingram calls a "short-story cycle," even though they are not all about the same characters.

Ingram defines such a cycle as "a book of short stories so linked to each other by their author that the reader's successive experience on various levels of the pattern of the whole significantly modifies his experience of each of the component parts."[2] The links among the stories in this cycle, however, do not result in the kind of narrative progression found in Sherwood Anderson's *Winesburg, Ohio* or James Joyce's *Dubliners,* which Ingram examines as prototypes of the genre, but rather as a progression based upon the slow and painful achievement of spiritual enlightenment, something like what the Christian believer experiences upon passing through the ritual of the Stations of the Cross, or, more appropriately in dealing with Salinger, of successive stages that a soul would pass through according to Vedantic teachings in at last escaping fleshly reincarnations. These stages are portrayed through a variety of characters at various points on the road to enlightenment, though it would be easily possible to assimilate all the stories into the Glass family saga. Seymour Glass is the central figure in "A Perfect Day for Bananafish," as his sister Boo Boo (Beatrice) is in "Down at the Dinghy." The dead lover Walt, who is given no last name in "Uncle Wiggily in Connecticut," dies in the same fashion as the later identified Walt Glass, and Buddy Glass later claims the authorship of "Teddy." The mysterious Sergeant X in "For Esmé—with Love and Squalor," has wartime experiences like those of Seymour and Buddy Glass, though Seymour is dead and Buddy unmarried at the time of the story. The principal characters in "Just before the War with the Eskimos," "The Laughing Man," and "De Daumier-Smith's Blue Period" have similar sensibilities to the Glass family's; and the depraved characters in "Pretty Mouth and Green My Eyes" resemble Lane Coutell in "Franny" and Seymour's wife Muriel—the closest figures to villains in the tales later assigned to Buddy. Since Buddy is credited with the first and the last in the cycle, there is no reason one cannot work on the assumption that he was responsible also for drawing on his siblings and acquaintances for the intervening tales. Certainly the stories amount to a progressive account of a matter that much concerned him in the later Glass family stories—nine crucial stages in the purification of the lust- and ego-ridden soul from the torments of the earthly wasteland as it strives to reach that ego-free state in which it may be absorbed at last into *the* One.

I tread dangerous ground here. The unsympathetic and insensitive will leap at once to the conclusion that I am claiming that Salinger sat down one fine day while perfecting the final version of *Catcher* and quite consciously plotted some architectonic disaster like the Paris Pompidou Center, which he then proceeded to execute over five years before he fled to the sanctuary of the New Hampshire hills.

Nothing of the kind. If he had, the whole project would probably have been as disastrous as nineteenth-century efforts like Joanna Baillie's to write series of plays illustrating the passions or seven deadly sins or what have you. Authors intent on the always excruciating task of capturing their vision in words may work unaware of subtle forces that influence their efforts. Salinger need not have preconceived some overall design for the stories, nor may he even have detected it in the completed work. Rather, as the successive stories led him to ponder the stages in a process that intrigued him, he could have moved from a contemplation of the presentation of one problem to the succeeding one. Certainly the reader's experience may be enriched by the perception of even unpremeditated relationships.

"A Perfect Day for Bananafish"

The story that opens the collection has achieved such a reputation of its own as one of the best-known American stories of the years since World War II that it has rarely been considered in conjunction with the other stories in the book, though it has been endlessly discussed as the springboard for the later tales about the meteoric career and spectacular death of its principal character, Seymour Glass.

Although readers will continue to discover private meanings for such a vivid tale, there is really nothing inscrutable about the surface narrative. Army veteran Seymour Glass has recently been released from a military hospital, where he had been under psychiatric care. Over his in-laws' objections, he has driven his wife Muriel to a Florida seashore resort for her first vacation in years. While the highly self-possessed Muriel talks on the telephone to her overly solicitous mother, Seymour meets four-or-five-year-old Sybil Carpenter on the beach about a quarter of a mile from the hotel. After some childlike conversation, Seymour takes Sybil into the water on an inflated rubber float and tells her the tragic story of the bananafish who die of banana fever after swimming into a hole and gorging themselves on so many bananas that they cannot get out. When Sybil reports she sees one of the fish with six bananas in its mouth, Seymour hurries her back to the beach and returns to his hotel, where he scolds a startled woman on the elevator for looking at his feet. Arriving at his hotel room, where Muriel is now sleeping on one twin bed, he sits down on the other and shoots himself through the right temple with an Ortgies caliber 7.65 automatic.

Seymour's bananafish fable has been given a great many plausible and fantastic readings; but on a literal level, it is clear that since Seymour is the only character besides the bananafish who dies in the story, and since he has brought a suicide weapon with him, he identifies with the fish and the fever that kills them. The third-person narrator (much later identified as Seymour's brother Buddy) never discusses Seymour's motivation; but even though the suicide comes with startling suddenness, it is not really surprising. Seymour is reported to have wrecked a car recently by driving it into some trees, and a psychiatrist has told Muriel's parents that he might lose control of himself completely. He is a sick man, who conceals a nonexistent tattoo; and the story is entirely successful as a minutely detailed account of a psychotic's predictable and foreshadowed self-destruction. This crafted accomplishment is not enough to account, however, for the most haunting features of the story—the bananafish allegory or Seymour's calling his cool and rather brave wife (she did let him drive the car despite the earlier accident) "Miss Spiritual Tramp of 1948" and other slurs that are not disclosed, partly because she did not learn German in order to read a book of poems he had given her by the "only great poet of the century" (almost certainly Rainer Maria Rilke, who is praised elsewhere in Salinger's writings).

Ten years after Seymour's debut in the *New Yorker*, Salinger had his fictional alter ego, Seymour's brother Buddy, explain, seemingly belatedly in "Seymour: An Introduction" in the same periodical that "the true artist-seer [as he identifies Seymour], the heavenly fool who can and does produce beauty, is mainly dazzled to death by his own scruples, the blinding shapes and colors of his own sacred human conscience."[3] Critics, and even Buddy himself, have pointed out that Seymour in the two stories is not exactly the same person, so that it may be misleading to read this later explanation back into the earlier story, particularly since the original portrayal of Muriel reflects Buddy's rather than Seymour's opinion of her.

In my earlier book about Salinger, I argued that Seymour committed suicide in order to make the well-composed Muriel pay attention to him, but I now think this explanation vastly oversimplifies the situation. I would still argue that Seymour is like the kind of petulant child who demands that adults—and playmates—pay constant attention to him or her. If such children do not attract the kind of attention they crave, they devise constantly more conspicuous and dangerous ways to win the coveted notice (like Seymour's charges against the inoffensive woman on the elevator just before his suicide). Shouting, "look at me, look at me," they climb further and further up the tree, out on a limb, run faster and faster without watching where they are going, showing off how long they can hold on to the lit firecracker. The most aggressive may harm others, but usually these exhibitionists injure only themselves physically. Ignoring them does not make them stop, but only incites them to act more hysterically.

I would argue now, however, that Seymour blames the situation less on the insufficiently appreciative Muriel than, in light of the bananafish analogy, upon himself, for succumbing to materialistic temptations.

To begin with his diagnosis of banana fever, we may observe that bananas have two associations that cannot be ignored when they are used as symbols in a story about a struggle between materialism and spirituality. Literally, they are not only fattening, but golden colored (emblems of wealthy hedonism); in the vulgarest kind of symbolism, they are phalluses (one of the most hilarious examples of Hollywood's slipping something past the censors in the days of the production code was Carmen Miranda's banana routine in the wartime film *The Gang's All Here*).

Salinger would have been working on "A Perfect Day for Bananafish" during the same period that he was working out the final version of *Catcher*. Both contain important climactic interviews between a very young girl and a deeply disturbed young man. In *Catcher*, Holden gives up his dream of serving as a catcher in the rye when he sees his sister Phoebe, like the other kids, grabbing for the phony gold rings on the carousel. Seymour, who has said that he likes blue bathing suits (the traditional color of innocence) is reminded that Sybil's is yellow. He has *not*, however, said that hers is blue. He says, "That's a fine bathing suit you have on. If there's one thing I like, it's a blue bathing suit."[4] When reminded that hers is yellow, he observes, "What a fool I am."

Then when Sybil reports seeing a bananafish with six fruit in its mouth, Seymour makes a traditional act of obeisance by kissing her foot and rushes her back to the shore without explanation, although Salinger interjects here a rare comment on the characters' feelings, when he states that Sybil runs off "without regret" (17). Seymour's actions, like his others, is not explained, but it seems parallel to Holden's resignation at the end of *Catcher* to letting kids alone, if they must fall off the merry-go-round. His bananafish story has not inspired in Sybil compassion for the fish's plight, but the same materialistic vision he associates with Muriel. Holden's discovery quiets him, but Seymour's further disillusionment with the next generation could be an important reason why this "perfect day for bananfish" is the moment for leaving a world that may hold nothing for him but more years in a psychiatric hospital. This difference in the characters' sensibilities suggests a strong reason why Salinger may have been writing his last words about the character who had dominated his vision during the first stage of his writing (Holden) during the same period when he was discov-

ering the character who would dominate rhe rest of his active publishing career (Seymour). The unmystical Holden has given up any
aspiration to exercise his messianic tendencies; but Seymour, perceiving himself in relation to both Muriel and Sybil as a failed guru, is
distressed beyond endurance, as shown by his irrational outburst
against the terrified woman in the elevator.

The perception of Seymour as a failed guru provides the starting
point for an analysis of the nine collected stories as a short story cycle.
The key to such a coherent interpretation of the collection is Hamayun
Mirza's unpublished explanation that despite the value that Seymour
and his teachings provide as examples for his sibling-disciples, he is
from the traditional Vedantic point of view a failed guru.[5] This is because he has not been able to overcome the negative karma that he has
accumulated because of his inability to transcend the temptations of
the flesh that preclude the attainment of *mukti,* which Salinger's
teacher Swami Nikhilananda describes as "liberation from perfection,
bondage, separateness, misery, and death."[6]

The real clue to the motivation for Scymour's suicide is found not
in "Bananafish" or the later Glass family stories, but in the last of the
nine collected stories, "Teddy," when the title character, who is a true
guru because of his ability to transcend his human incarnations and
achieve liberation from the cycles of death and rebirth, explains to
slow-learning educator Bob Nicholson that in Teddy's previous incarnation he was "making a very nice spiritual advancement," when "I
met a lady, and sort of stopped meditating." He does also explain that
he had not been sufficiently far enough advanced that he could have
gone straight to Brahma if he had not met that lady, but at least, as
he puts it, "I wouldn't have had to get incarnated in an American
body. . . . I mean it's very hard to meditate and live a spiritual life in
America" (188). Seymour resembles the previous incarnation of Teddy
McArdle. His meeting with Muriel halted his proper spiritual development. Although he might not have been spiritually advanced
enough in any event to go straight to Brahma from his American incarnation, once he has discovered that he is going no further in this
incarnation, he becomes frustrated about living purposelessly and seeks
to accelerate the process by destroying this failed flesh and proceeding
to another incarnation in which he hopes to do better.

Teddy, of course, could not have been Seymour's reincarnation, since
he was born on Valentine's Day in 1942 (though this is less than four
months before Seymour's marriage). Salinger is, however, not provid-

ing an episodic history of the progress of one soul but an account of the process of spiritualization and the obstacles to it, especially in the United States, through portrayals of representative types, which, as already cautioned, he most likely did not preconceive as forming a collective history. *Nine Stories* compresses a series of stages in the soul's advancement into a briefer period than would be possible for any one; a perfectly acceptable procedure because the progress of any soul is emblematic of the progress of all. With the effacement of a soul as the illusory person of Seymour Glass, however, we are at the beginning of a process that will end with the liberation of Teddy McArdle.

"Uncle Wiggily in Connecticut"

The point of the second of the nine stories lies in the answer to the dejected Eloise's rhetorical question "I was a nice girl, wasn't I?" (38). In my earlier book, I used "Uncle Wiggily in Connecticut" as a key work to interpret Salinger's vision, because it was the one that offered in the fewest pages contrasting glimpses of the two worlds—the "nice" and the "phony"—with which he was principally concerned. The following remarks in no way refute or replace that earlier argument, which still provides a useful approach to the satirical portrayal of American life that is a persisting element throughout Salinger's writing; but I am here interested in the way in which this story also serves as a building block in the particular structure in which it appears.

The six stories from this one to "Pretty Mouth and Green My Eyes" all portray responses that individuals make to the inevitability of having to cope with the phony world that Salinger, like both Holden Caulfield and Seymour Glass, despises. "Uncle Wiggily in Connecticut" is, like "A Perfect Day for Bananafish," the tale of a defeat. Seymour Glass has found himself unable to cope with the phony world and opts out. Suicide may not, however, always be a possible or acceptable alternative to dealing with disillusionment. Eloise in "Uncle Wiggily" is not driven to death by what she encountered in life, but she is reduced to a kind of death-in-life that has withered her into a cold, high-handed, alienated being.

The title "Uncle Wiggily in Connecticut" places in ironic juxtaposition the "nice" world that Holden Caulfield sought in vain and the "phony" world that surrounded him. Eloise lived briefly in a "nice" world, when she first arrived in the East from the Wild West of Boise, Idaho (the country to which Holden dreamed of escaping), while she enjoyed a brief, idyllic romance with a soldier named Walt, whose last name is never disclosed in the story, but who turns out in "Zooey" to have been one of the Glass children. Walt had called her injured ankle "Uncle Wiggily" after the kindly, old rabbit in Howard Garis's children's stories who goes about solving other's painful problems. This "Uncle Wiggily," however, is trapped in Connecticut (where Salinger was living when the story was published), which is depicted as foul a place as one could conceive on a dreary icy day when everything is going wrong.

Eloise is reduced to a state that makes her spitefully cruel to her maid and young daughter because Walt had been killed during the war, not in combat, but in a senseless accident while trying to pack a carelessly handled stove for shipment home by a looting officer, and she has married a man who won her by telling her that Jane Austen was his favorite author when he had not even read her novels.

The spirit of the former "nice" girl has been reincarnated in her nearly blind daughter, Salinger's more successful version of Raymond Ford in "The Inverted Forest," who lives almost entirely in her imagination. After Eloise's nasty drunken effort to snap Ramona back to reality by trying to force her to give up her fantasies about imaginary "boy friends," the mother is suddenly stricken by a realization of what has happened to her and begins to cry along with her devastated daughter before going downstairs to plead with an old college roommate to tell her that she had once been "a nice girl." Her prospects are as dark as this fouled, wintry day in Connecticut; but she can find some small comfort in memories as she repeats over and over, "Poor Uncle Wiggily," crying uncontrollably over her daughter's thick glasses.

"Just before the War with the Eskimos"

The third of the collected stories is the first not to be associated, even by afterthought, with the Glass family, though Franny could easily be substituted for Ginnie Maddox, the principal figure in "Just before the War with the Eskimos," whose exquisite sensibility made her unable to dispose of her dead Easter chick for three days. (Chicken sandwiches also figure in the tales both women dominate.) Ginnie is still a "nice girl," who is able to make the kind of spontaneous gesture that Eloise has hardened herself against; but she is surrounded by characters already lost to the "phony" world, and she is already beginning to display traits like the mature Muriel Glass's cattiness toward other women.

Ginnie finally sees the light, however, and decides that she can not only forgive the petty debt another girl owes her, but try to be a better friend to this lonely Selena, whom she has previously "openly considered . . . the biggest drip at Miss Basehoar's—a school ostensibly abounding with fair-sized drips" (39).

Selena's problem is her brother Franklin (no self-made man), one of the most ineffectual characters in Salinger's oeuvre, who wears glasses and has extremely poor posture, as well as a weak heart that has kept him out of the armed services in World War II, which he had to spend distastefully working in an aircraft factory in Ohio. Although he moans as if wounded in battle about a cut finger, he has no Band-Aids, because he is the type that would never have a Band-Aid around for any of the wounds that life inflicts.

He and Ginnie get off to a bad start after unexpectedly encountering each other (she has not even known Selena has a brother) when he denounces her sister as a snob, though she secretly shares his opinion that her sister is conceited about her good looks, and she is touched when he offers her half of a chicken sandwich, although she only takes a bite out of it.

Her sympathies are most stirred, however, when she discovers that Franklin faces a further problem of the greatest gravity among those few nice folks on Salinger's tight little island. The author bombards the reader with every signal in stock that Franklin, despite his inadequacies, is heterosexual. Franklin provides, in fact, the bizarre title for the story when denouncing the old guys "around sixty," who are sending the crowds on the street below back to "the goddam draftboard" for the upcoming war with the Eskimos. When Ginnie carelessly lets slip, "*You* wouldn't have to go anyway," she realizes "before the statement was completely out that she was saying the wrong thing" (49). His animus against Ginnie's sister Joan, who is now marrying a lieutenant commander in the navy, is that she never answered any of "eight goddam letters" that he wrote to her, because he never had the nerve to call her up. His failure with her is apparently typical of his relations with the opposite sex, for he had been reduced to depending for companionship upon a man named Eric, whom he met while working in Ohio.

While Salinger allows Holden Caulfield to point out "flits" in

Catcher (186, 194), as third-person narrator he never applies the term
to Eric; but he drops clues that make it impossible to consider Eric as
anything but a homosexual. He raves on after meeting Ginnie about
"this awful little person from Al*too*na, Pennsylvania—or *one* of those
places," who has been sharing his apartment for months and then walks
out early one morning "taking with him anything and everything he
can lay his filthy, dirty hands on" (51–52). Then when she asks him if
he spent the war working in the aircraft plant because he has a bad
heart, too, he cuts short his answer, but not before revealing, "Heav-
ens, no. . . . I have the constitution of——" (54), not leaving many
plausible explanations for his 4-F status. As lagniappe, Salinger has
Eric throw in that he is trying to get Franklin, whose taste runs to he-
man gangster films and westerns, to see Jean Cocteau's *Beauty and the
Beast*, a cult favorite of gay audiences. (Franklin and Eric may derive
their names from Franklin Pangborn and Eric Blore, comic character
actors who played effeminate roles in Astaire-Rogers films and many
others of the 1930s.)

Ginnie's compassion has not developed to the point of extending to
Eric, for she leaves without saying goodbye; but she has changed her
attitude toward her "drippy" classmate. She has made a start toward a
selfless consideration of others that marks a spiritual advancement over
the tearful state of the regretful Eloise.

"The Laughing Man"

"The Chief," as football player and law student John Gedsudski of
Staten Island is called by his idolizing charges in "The Laughing Man,"
fourth story in Salinger's collection, is made of tougher stuff than Ginnie and illustrates the more painful achievement of transcending his
own defeat in order to force others toward enlightenment.

"The Laughing Man" of the title is one of the Chief's fanciful inven-
tions to entertain the "Comanches," twelve upper middle-class disci-
ples, who are sons of Manhattan apartment dwellers. One of them
narrates the story about the Chief's supervision of their afternoon and
weekend recreation. "The Laughing Man" also serves evidently as a
kind of wish-fulfillment figure for the powerful but somewhat dwarf-
like chief, a Robin Hood who hides a misshapen visage behind a
poppy-petal mask.

All goes well with this arrangement until the Chief begins an affair
with a beautiful Wellesley girl who wears a beaver coat and who finally

ingratiates herself enough with the woman-shy preteenagers to be allowed to play in their baseball games. Something the young narrator (who in age and temperament might be Buddy Glass) cannot understand, however, breaks up the romance. After Mary Hudson, the girl, walks away for the last time, the Chief ends the Arabian-nights-like tale of "The Laughing Man" by describing this heroic figure's wasting away to death after achieving a fantastic revenge on the father-and-daughter detective team who are his principal pursuers. The youngest boy on the bus is reduced to tears and even the tougher nine-year-old narrator's teeth chatter when he sees flapping around a lamppost a piece of red paper that resembles a poppy-petal mask. The Comanches continue their games under the Chief's tutelage but the story is never resumed.

The story appears more meaningful as part of a story cycle than as an autonomous work, because it is difficult to interpret it in isolation as more than the account of a disillusioning experience, an inevitable part of the narrator's growing up, like Holden's loss of his vision at the end of *Catcher* or the chastening epiphany of the young narrator's folly at the end of James Joyce's "Araby."

Richard Allan Davison has made the only significant effort to find more in the story than a juvenile rite of passage; but his efforts are frustrated by the lack of any information about the nature of the attraction between the Chief and Mary.[7] If Salinger does provide the reader with any clues to the Chief's life away from his Comanche tribe, they are sublimated in the story-within-a-story the Chief tells the boys drawing vaguely on Victor Hugo's Gothic fantasy *L'Homme qui rit*. Without going into all the lurid details that Salinger lovingly summarizes from the preposterous tale, we may join the story session with the last episode in which the title character is caught in "a physical and intellectual trap" set by a famous detective and his daughter. When the Laughing Man unmasks, the father has averted his head because of a coughing spell; but the daughter passes out from her shock at the sight of Laughing Man's face. This installment ends as the Chief goes for his final interview with Mary. When the story resumes after this meeting, the Laughing Man gives the Dufarges (as the detectives are called) a terrible surprise when, after having four bullets fired pointblank into him, he manages to regurgitate them fastidiously into the pair who drop dead at his feet.

Davison may underrate "the social class differences" between the lovers as the reason for their breakup. Though Mary's father is never mentioned in the frame narrative, the presence of a daughter in the inset tale is a bit odd, so that it seems possible that the Chief is using his fantastic narrative to objectify his own problems with his girl's disapproving father. If this is the situation, Gedsudski would be, like Salinger himself, introducing his audience into the phoniness of WASP society, further strengthening the impression that the young narrator could be the impressionable Buddy Glass. But the real point of the story would remain that the Chief was not, like Seymour, driven to suicide by his defeat; rather he used it to give his young charges a startling object lesson in not expecting too much from life.

"Down at the Dinghy"

If class bias is the underlying subject of "The Laughing Man," the story clearly fits into a pattern of portraying those forces that are negative to the liberation of the soul in American society, moving from bigotry toward "unmanliness" in "Just before the War with the Eskimos" to discrimination against "lower-class" ethnic stocks (Chief Gedsudski's name shows that he comes from an Eastern European immigrant background) to the viciousness of race hatred still flourishing in the United States after the World War II victory over the Nazis abroad in "Down at the Dinghy," the fifth of the nine stories. It clearly belongs to the Glass family history through its introduction of Seymour and Buddy's sister Boo Boo and her young son Lionel, the only third-generation Glass that readers ever meet.

The story is also the most contrived and unconvincing in the collection, making one speculate that its shortcomings may have been a reason for its original appearance as Salinger's only contribution to *Harper's,* whereas all the other Glass family stories appeared in the *New Yorker.* Faced with an aberration like the racial prejudice that had resulted in the Holocaust, Salinger seemed, as in "A Girl I Knew," unable to come up with an adequately harrowing example of this soul's illness (as he does in "Pretty Mouth and Green My Eyes") and to have had to fall back on cute sentimentality. The matter at issue here may provide the measure of the limits of his ability to stare unblinkingly at the human condition and account in part for his flight to the woods.

The result in "A Girl I Knew" was a wistfully nostalgic tale about a lost world, well suited for a family magazine; but his story cycle demands stories with the stunning impact of "A Perfect Day for Bananafish," "Uncle Wiggily in Connecticut," and "For Esmé." "Down at the Dinghy," by contrast, approaches its revelation of squalor so trepidatiously that often recent readers even miss its point.

What it does provide in the development of the cycle is a figure who is able to transcend squalor and survive in the midst of it better than Ginnie Maddox or the deflated Chief Gedsudski. Even in his portrayal of Boo Boo Glass Tannenbaum, however, Salinger forces judgments on the reader in a way that he seldom does, for they should be left to judge for themselves that she is "a stunning and final girl" (77), whatever this puzzling phrase may mean.

It is also not clear just what she does to change her hypersensitive four-year-old son Lionel's mind about running away, for she never does anything to straighten out the farfetched misunderstanding that prompts his resolution. It takes a really huge suspension of disbelief to accept that a bright and inquisitive child of four could think a servant was saying "kite" when she was saying "kike"; and even if we accept this possibility for the sake of the moral to come, one wonders if a kid with such a finicky sensibility could be protected from all the bruises a hard world may inflict. As I earlier argued, a kid who defined a *kite* as "one of those things that go up in the *air* . . . with *string* you hold" (86) could have feared that a father to whom he was much attached might break loose and get lost in the sky; but it is still not clear why Lionel would believe his mother when she tells him they will go to the train station and get Daddy and bring him home when the boy has not responded to her earlier overtures.

Salinger is relying too heavily in the story on readers' reacting to a coarse, grumbling domestic servant's use of the opprobrious term *kike*, as John Edward Hardy does when he describes the story in a collection designed for German students concerned with "the social problem of anti-semitism in the United States."[8] While encountering the term may upset readers, nothing happens that enlightens Lionel about the actual situation confronting him. Boo Boo has only deferred a crisis, not confronted it, so this remains the story of a temporary tranquilizing and does not present lasting resolution of the kind Salinger imagines in the next story. Certainly in this sense Boo Boo does not here prove herself to be the kind of "final girl" that Esmé is.

It is also perhaps indicates that Americans have at least polished the veneer over ineradicably deep-set prejudices enough so that many recent students do not get the point of the story at all without awkward explanations, since the degrading epithet applied here to Jews is no longer a familiar word. The story has thus become more dated than

most of Salinger's works, although the underlying problem that it deals
with has not necessarily diminished.

"For Esmé—with Love and Squalor"

The sixth in the collection of nine stories remains one of Salinger's
most admired works. Despite its use of a World War II setting, it
remains, as Ihab Hassan calls it, "a modern epithalamium," a celebra-
tion of the rite of marriage.[9] It depicts the love the narrator feels for
one he recalls as an ideal woman and human being and the squalor she
requests in a story she claims she would be flattered to have him write
exclusively for her. I find no reason today to change what I said in
praise of this story twenty-five years ago, except to place it within the
larger context of its eight companion pieces.

In the first of two scenes, a titled English girl of about thirteen,
whom the narrator has observed singing at a local choir rehearsal in the
British town where he is stationed with the American army, sufficiently overcomes her aristocratic reserve to approach him in a tearoom.
She displays a great knack for "keeping count" of things, a desire to
train herself to be more compassionate, and a contempt for Americans,
since most she has met "act like animals." When she learns the narrator
is a writer, she asks to write the story about "squalor," with which he
ruefully admits he is becoming steadily better acquainted.

They are joined after a few minutes by Esmé's five-year-old brother
Charles, who laughs uproariously at his own riddles, but who himself
acts like an animal when the narrator beats him to the punch line the
second time he poses the same riddle. Esmé admits he has a violent
temper but at the end of the interview she manages to drag him back
to kiss the narrator (as decorum would not permit her to do). When
the narrator poses the same riddle again and permits the boy to deliver
the punch line, Charles rushes from the room "possibly in hysterics."
Esmé then makes a more formal and courteous departure, expressing
the hope that the narrator may return from the war, in which she and
Charles have lost their father, with all his "faculties intact."

In the second scene, the narrator, now for unfathomable reasons mas-
querading as Sergeant X, has indeed become acquainted with the squalor that he proceeds to chronicle. Possibly to illustrate Esmé's charge
that Americans act like animals, which the narrator had chided as
snobbish, Salinger exhibits the most grotesque array of insensitive ego-

tists possibly ever summoned up in so few words. To set the tone, there is the lingering ghost of the vicious Nazi misanthrope, Joseph Goebbels, in a copy of whose book *The Time Without Parallel,* a Nazi spinster, whose former room Sergeant X occupies, has scrawled, "Dear God, life is hell." The sergeant glosses this with another from Dostoyevski's *Brothers Karamazov* about hell being "the suffering of being unable to love" (105).

That the spirit of Goebbels has not been vanquished is demonstrated by the Yankees who have ended his loveless "time" displaying the same kind of ugly behavior. A sadistic letter from Sergeant X's older brother requests "a couple of bayonets or swastikas" for his kids (106). The sergeant tears it up and throws the pieces into a wastebasket into which he later vomits, but he cannot so easily escape the squalor personified by the "photogenic" Corporal Z, from whom we learn that Sergeant X has just been released from a hospital (of the kind where Seymour Glass had also been a patient) after a nervous breakdown.

The corporal, whose first name is Clay (inert, lumpen, echoing one of the most squalid tales in James Joyce's *Dubliners* story cycle), brings news of the officious Bulling, who forces underlings to travel at inconvenient hours in order to impress them with his authority, and of Clay's girlfriend Loretta, a psychology major who blames Sergeant X's breakdown not on wartime experiences but on lifelong instability, yet excuses Clay's sadistic killing of a cat as "temporary insanity."

The most squalid is Clay himself, who is too obtuse even to recognize criticism. When Sergeant X is exasperated beyond his usual reserve into a rare outburst of truth by Clay's insistence on dwelling upon his shooting a cat, the sergeant makes it clear that he thinks Clay has been "brutal," "cruel," and "dirty"; but Clay, who thinks Eisenhower jackets *are* good because they *look* good, only asks why the sergeant cannot be "sincere" (110).

When Clay leaves, Sergeant X—who has thought better of apologizing to the corporal—is too disturbed to type a letter that might have had some therapeutic value. He closes his eyes, and upon reopening them finds a package that has been tracking him for about a year. Esmé has sent him her father's watch, which she hopes he will accept as "a lucky talisman." There follows a postscript of ten "hellos" from Charles, whom Esmé is "teaching to read and write and . . . finding an extremely intelligent novice" (113). This unexpected demonstration of unadulterated affection redeems the sergeant from his private hell and allows him to go to sleep (the usual signal of the resolution of a problem in the Glass family stories), feeling that he may yet come through the war with his "faculties intact."

"For Esmé—with Love and Squalor" is thus a dramatic gloss on the Dostoyevski quotation that the trembling sergeant writes in Goebbels's book. Just before the appearance of his much acclaimed novel, *The Catcher in the Rye,* Salinger succeeded in personifying through Esmé and Corporal Clay prototypical representatives of the "nice" and "phony" worlds—the "love" and "squalor" of the title.

The story thus read in isolation is a magnificent tribute to the "stiff upper lip," the self-discipline, that is the most glorious tradition of the British aristocracy. Esmé has suffered not only the privations and dislocations of war, but has also lost both parents as a teenager and has been prematurely saddled with worrisome responsibilities. Through all this she seeks to train herself to be more compassionate and displays her achievement in her timely gift to Sergeant X.

In terms of the story cycle as a whole, Esmé embodies the highest potential of the human being who chooses to remain firmly earthbound within a squalid society, struggling against the obstacles created by creatures like Goebbels and his American counterparts to develop compassion and display it to her family, to a lonely American soldier, and through the marriage that provides the occasion for telling this story from the past to her society and to the future generations, whose faculties she may help keep intact. Esmé differs from both the defeated Seymour Glass and the transcendent Teddy McArdle in that she remains resolutely in Holden Caulfield's world without being corrupted by its "phoniness" or resigning herself to putting up with things as they are. Her story is one of the rare ones of the victory of the "nice" world over the "phony."

Esmé much resembles Boo Boo Glass in "Down in the Dinghy," but she is in a position to exercise much wider influence for the good. The story is also a much greater artistic achievement, because instead of simply presenting a mature woman whose attributes we must accept on the author's authority, readers can witness the struggle of a shy and nervous teenager (despite her composure, she has bitten her fingernails to the quick) to achieve this highest human potential. It is noteworthy that to give dramatic life to this figure, Salinger found it necessary to leave the United States of his other stories and find his model among the British aristocracy.

"Pretty Mouth and Green My Eyes"

We have followed the human spirit in this story cycle through six stages in the loss and development of compassion, arriving with Esmé at the pinnacle of mortal expectations. This is, however, a perilously unstable peak. It may seem curious to find Salinger following up a story of a triumph of human good will by plunging us precipitately into the pit of the modern urban hell, but in one of his most bitter, cynical stories, he shows that he could work in the manner of other *New Yorker* writers like John O'Hara and John Cheever on the rare occasions he chose. He had not written a story about the fashionable world where—as Paul Levine wryly quips—adult is equated with adultery, however, since his short early work, "Go See Eddie," in which a concerned brother tries to extricate his sister from a succession of sordid affairs.

One obvious link, however, between "For Esmé" and the following story, "Pretty Mouth and Green My Eyes," is that the latter could certainly be the tale of squalor that Esmé requested the American soldier to write (it is the only one of the nine stories that did not feature at least one member of the Glass family, but it is certainly about the kind of people they would have observed and detested).

A more important connection between the two stories, however, is that in the ordering of the nine stories "Pretty Mouth and Green My Eyes" reminds us how precarious is the balance that permits one to function within a contaminated world without being destroyed by it. Sergeant X might have encountered someone like the cuckolded Arthur's wife Joanie as easily as the spiritually redemptive Esmé. ("Pretty Mouth and Green My Eyes" is, among other things, a modern variant, as the betrayed Arthur's name suggests, on the popular Camelot story, not long afterward to find its American embodiment in the rise and fall of President John Kennedy.) A specific connection is even made between the two stories by the "immense green eyes" of Esmé's brother Charles and the "stone dead" eyes of the wife in "Pretty Mouth" that the spellbound husband had once supposed green.

Charles, still in his barbarously unlettered state, says his eyes are orange, the fiery color of the sun; but they are truly green—appropriate to an epithalamium that honors the fertile season of spring. Joanie's eyes in the other story, however, prove not to be this promising green, but the wintry death color of "goddam *sea* shells" (125). The story of

Esmé and Charles is of victory over squalor; "Pretty Mouth and Green My Eyes," on the other hand, describes the victory of squalor. Concluding with one of Salinger's most adroit uses of the surprise ending, it is not, however, like some of his apprentice pieces, merely tricky trivia; it compresses into an uninterrupted account of a few minutes of pathetic self-revelation all that Esmé would need to know of squalor to understand why some people might seek to avoid any responsibility for the modern world or even any active association with it. The story is about a betrayed man who is driven unbeknownst to him to the humiliating defeat of lying to the one person who would know that he is lying, a supposed friend and colleague who is cuckolding him. The extreme impersonality of the narration suggests indeed a fastidious sensibility's revulsion at a world in which it does not wish to be immersed. This story indeed, which first appeared the same week in July 1951 that *The Catcher in the Rye* was published, reads like the author's curse on a world he would soon leave behind for the hills of New Hampshire.

Many story cycles about our modern world might have ended on this deflating note. Indeed James Joyce's prototypical *Dubliners* ends with "The Dead," a depressing picture of a decayed society being buried under the purifying oblivion of a blanket of snow. Salinger, however, having plunged from a portrayal of the best that the material world can offer to the deepest pit of despair and deceit, was not content—as Holden Caulfield seems to have been at the end of *The Catcher in the Rye*—to abandon his quest hopelessly. The last two of the nine stories portray a rapid ascent that takes a disenchanted spirit at last out of this world altogether; the collection concludes with a mystical vision in the shaping of which both the garden of earthly delights revealed beneath a wartorn world in "For Esmé" and the mortal hell of "Pretty Mouth and Green My Eyes" both fade into illusions to be transcended.

"De Daumier-Smith's Blue Period"

The eighth story in Salinger's collection still remains after more than three decades his least adequately appreciated. Indeed one still finds that some readers have not yet discovered that it did not appear for the first time in *Nine Stories,* but that "De Daumier-Smith's Blue Period" is the only story of Salinger's known to have been first published outside the United States—in London's *World Review* in May 1952. It is not likely that we will find out why it first appeared abroad, but one may suspect that American editors in the 1950s may have had the same problems understanding this rambling confession that readers have since.

While once again we will probably never be sure, the story appears to be the first that Salinger completed after the publication of *The Catcher in the Rye*. It takes off in a new direction from the previous seven stories in the 1953 collection, but it does have a significant affinity with *Catcher* because the key decision that the pseudonymous artist makes in the short story closely resembles Holden's final decision that kids have to be left alone to pursue their own destinies and take their own risks. De Daumier-Smith decides that he must give Sister Irma "her freedom to follow her own destiny." Similarly his enigmatic conclusion, "Everybody is a nun" (164), may be a more lyrical way of phrasing Holden Caulfield's discovery that if you tell anybody anything, "you start missing everybody" (277), because everybody, like a nun, is a bride of heaven who should share in universal compassion.

Jean de Daumier-Smith may thus offer clues to the behavior of a somewhat more mature Holden, although there are two important differences between them as they reach their nonjudgmental attitudes toward the sacredness of all human beings (an attitude also expressed in Seymour Glass's diary in "Raise High the Roof Beam, Carpenters"). Holden, as we have seen, has a completely unmystical sensibility; De Daumier-Smith, on the other hand, cannot, as he would like, "if possible," dismiss the possibility that his "quite transcendent" experience is "a borderline case, of genuine mysticism" (163). His experience at the shop window of "enamel urinals and bedpans, with a sightless wooden dummy-deity standing by in a marked-down rupture truss" (157) transformed into "a shimmering field of exquisite, twice-blessed, enamel flowers" (164) is inexplicable except as a mystical experience. Indeed, the passage is certainly one of the closest any writer has come to translating into words such an ineffable experience (Salinger provides a more powerful sense of the impact of the experience, for example, than Allen Ginsberg in his recollections of his visions of William Blake).[10]

The difficulty with "De Daumier-Smith's Blue Period" is that Salinger does succeed in transcending the logic that Teddy McArdle protests against in the final story of the collection, and few readers have been able to make the trip with him. (A lot of "tripping" was, of course, done with artificial stimulants by Salinger's contemporaries— one matter of which he never speaks at all, though any kind of drug use seems utterly out of keeping with all that we are told about the

Glass family—but self-engendered symbolic transcendence appears rare even during the flourishing of meditation movements.) Gwynn and Blotner's pioneering critique of Salinger includes what remains the best humanistic reading of the story, but they conclude that "it can hardly escape the label of *tour de force*," because it is more than a humanistic story.[11] Its mysterious narrator has moved beyond the limits of Holden Caulfield's earthbound vision.

A second point about the story that marks the movement of its author's understanding beyond *Catcher*, but that renders "De Daumier-Smith" within *Nine Stories* only a prelude to the climactic "Teddy" is that its narrator moves into the transfigured realm beyond time on this one occasion, but does not return there. As far as the story goes, his experience in Montreal is the extent of his mystical experience—something unsought that he does not seek to repeat. He comes back to earth to spend the rest of his summer girl-watching and then returns to school. He retains his emotions and leaves the timeless realm to Teddy McArdle. He has also learned how to control these emotions, so that he is a far more stable and self-confident person than Holden Caulfield. He returns to school without agonizing over whether he will apply himself or not; and he never does get in touch with Sister Irma again, although he is not shaken up by having to make such definite decisions.

Salinger has created in De Daumier-Smith a complementary figure to Holden; he displays a capacity to transcend the phony world, but chooses to remain in it, to make his own decisions and to stand by them. He is a kind of male counterpart to Boo Boo Glass; and despite the differences in his background he could easily be assimilated into the Glass family, though he is much less finicky than the brothers we come to know best.

The revelation he experiences at the end of the story is remarkably parallel to the one enjoyed decades earlier by Henry Fleming at the end of Stephen Crane's *Red Badge of Courage*, written at the very beginning of the period of modernist alienation that Salinger's work extends to its final stages. Crane depicts Henry as optimistically perceiving that "the world was a world for him though many discovered it to be made of oaths and walking-sticks."[12] Although the similarity seems certainly coincidental, it is noteworthy because so few other modernist protagonists—even in other works of Crane and Salinger—have experienced such self-confidently optimistic visions. Crane's perception of a world of "oaths and walking-sticks" closely resembles Salinger's image of the drab world of orthopedic appliances, although such images would be obvious to any writer seeking to give a sense of people's need for "crutches." Henry Fleming also has a transcendent vision, though without even the supernatural apparatus that Salinger summons up. Tough-minded Stephen Crane functioned always in the horizon-bound world of his "Open Boat." Fleming has shaken off the "crutches" offered by the establishments that seek to enslave the free spirit; but, within the first flush of a modernist emancipation that found its richest fulfillment in the works of James Joyce, Henry assumes that the world is "for him" in the most arrogantly possessive sense. Indeed we know from another story, "The Veteran," that Crane envisioned Henry living a life of his own choosing (though a modest one back on the farm) and dying at last a hero's death of his own choosing, which led to his transcendent immolation.[13]

"De Daumier-Smith's Blue Period" is an especially surprising complement to *Red Badge of Courage,* coming as it does near the end of the period of modernist alienation when disillusioned artists had generally lost faith in the possibility of self-fulfillment within the entropic limits of spaceship *Earth.* Instead they found escape from institutional entrapment only in the reassurance of a mystical vision like that of the Beat Generation, which made survival possible through freedom from the anguished pursuit of materialistic goals (as in "Pretty Mouth and Green My Eyes"). Salinger's story shows that there remains a possibility of surviving within the material world without becoming dehumanized. There remains even in the wasteland a possibility of innocence, but readers have a tough time recognizing it.

Just as Salinger might have ended his collection with "Pretty Mouth and Green My Eyes," so he might have ended it with De Daumier-Smith's benediction, which balances this book by providing an answer to Eloise's anguished cry in "Uncle Wiggily in Connecticut," "I was a nice girl, wasn't I?"— we have all been nice, "Everybody is a nun." Salinger, however, was not satisfied to find contentment in Connecticut. His collection did not begin with "Uncle Wiggily" but with "A Perfect Day For Bananafish." The unresolved matter of Seymour Glass remained. It was to absorb Salinger more and more exclusively for years into the future, but for the time its picture of the defeat the world inflicts on those uttering the "cries of pain" that Buddy Glass describes in "Seymour: An Introduction" (121) was to be balanced by the triumphant portrayal of the spirit that escapes this world for which it has ceased to care.

"Teddy"

The final story in the cycle has also raised problems; in fact, problems of such magnitude that even the sphinxlike author who has adamantly refused to discuss his works has obliquely funneled a response to critics of "Teddy" through his alter ego Buddy Glass. In "Seymour: An Introduction," Buddy claims responsibility for the story and describes it as "an exceptionally Haunting, Memorable, unpleasantly controversial, and throughly unsuccessful short story about a 'gifted' little boy aboard a transatlantic liner" (205). These remarks superficially describe "Teddy." Buddy/Salinger does not say why the story is considered unsuccessful, but one would suppose it was because readers publicized their missing its point, which Salinger had gone to elaborate pains to point out. The soundest course in dealing with this story, as with "Bananafish" (and many works by many writers that say what readers hope they are not hearing, like a discouraging medical diagnosis), is to take the words of such an outrageously candid character as Teddy McArdle at their face value.

Many readers have found the final sentence of the story and of the collection inscrutable: the none too quick-witted educator-interlocutor Nicholson is racing down to the ship's swimming pool after Teddy, "when he heard an all-piercing sustained scream—clearly coming from a small, female child. It was highly acoustical, as though it were reverberating within four tiled walls" (198). Nicholson is in such a hurry because a few minutes previously, Teddy, who, it is repeatedly hinted, has exhibited the gift of clairvoyance, has proposed the hypothesis that if, when in a few minutes he went down to the pool for his swimming lesson, it were empty, "my sister might come up and push me in. I could fracture my skull and die instantaneously." "That could happen," he continues, "My sister's only six, and she hasn't been a human being for very many lives, and she doesn't like me very much." But finally he challenges Nicholson, "What would be so tragic about it, though? . . . I'd just be doing what I was supposed to do, that's all, wouldn't I?" (193).

There do not really seem to be any problems about the interpretation of the story, but a lot about the response to it hinges on one's concept of the proper reply to Teddy's last question to Nicholson. Salinger leaves no doubt, however, that to Teddy the question is rhetorical. Earlier when Nicholson observed to Teddy, "you hold pretty firmly to the Vedantic theory of reincarnation," Teddy replied, "It isn't a theory, it's as much a part——" before Nicholson changes the subject (188). Teddy, before beginning the conversation with Nicholson, has written in his diary that "it [no referent supplied] will either happen today or February 14, 1958 when I am sixteen. It is ridiculous to mention even" (182), and he has frightened other people by warning them about times and places where they must be very careful. At the end of the unpleasant scene with his parents (who are much more like Holden Caulfield's than the Glass children's) that opens the story, Teddy, after watching some orange peels thrown from the ship float away and sink, observes, "After I go out this door, I may only exist in the minds of all my acquaintances. . . . I may be an orange peel" (173–74).

Nicholson finally decides that, believe in Vedantic reincarnation or not, he had better check out what is going on at the swimming pool; he arrives too late to tamper with fate, but then that is what is supposed to have happened.

The unstated issue here, of course, is that if Teddy foresees what his nasty little sister might do (not all little girls in Salinger's work are like Phoebe Caulfield or Esmé; Booper more nearly resembles the "no-neck" monsters yet to come in Tennessee William's 1955 play *Cat on a Hot Tin Roof*), he is, in effect, committing suicide, as Seymour Glass did, by letting her get away with it. From his own point of view, however, Teddy is simply a passive agent in an inevitable situation; he even denies feeling the "emotions" that would have influenced Seymour (186). To understand the story, one must get in rapport with the state of mind from which it was written. Doing so does not mean accepting the Vedantic concept or "believing" that Teddy's "visions" could mirror reality; it means only remaining open-minded enough to consider alternative explanations for events over those with which one has been indoctrinated. Teddy also tells Nicholson, "Most people don't want to see things the way they are. They don't even want to stop getting born and dying all the time" (191). Most occidental readers rationalize such an attitude as their Christian duty. Teddy's attitude, of course, may also be an extremely bright and hypersensitive young person's rationalization of his desire to escape from what he finds an intolerable situation. Even this interpretation, however, makes the story a devastating attack on American vulgarity—which most vulgarians will fiercely resent. No matter how one looks at the story, the point remains Teddy's that "most people don't want to see things the way they are."

Salinger's placement of this story within his cycle, however, suggests

that—consistent with his known interest in Vedantic doctrine and his
own partial withdrawal from the world—he sees in the culmination of
the soul's progress (what is called in Vedanta *mukti*) an escape from
gross materialism rather than the transcendence of physical surround-
ings achieved by Esmé and "De Daumier-Smith."

"Teddy" also leaves the impression, however, especially when compared with "A Perfect Day for Bananafish," that the author's view is
that one must accept passively the decrees of fate, which may not always coincide with one's personal wishes, as they do with Teddy's.
Seymour Glass's shortcoming, which many of Salinger's later stories
seek to justify or ameliorate, is that he did succumb to the very un-
spiritual tendency of impatiently lending a laggard fate a helping
hand. In his story Teddy explains to Nicholson that in his previous
incarnation he had been making satisfactory spiritual progress when a
lady caused his fall from grace and reincarnation in an American body.
Seymour has also experienced such a fall through his infatuation with
Muriel, whom he finally dubs "Miss Spiritual Tramp." Impatient,
however, with a life that has become pointless since another lies beyond
it, he speeds up what he hopes will be a more spiritually successful
incarnation; but in so doing, he provides no model for the god-seeker.
Teddy, however, provides a model of the proper path—one must overcome emotions altogether. "I don't see what they're *good* for" (186), he
tells Nicholson, because they are good only on this mortal sphere.
Teddy does love God, but not "sentimentally." One's thoughts dart
back to Salinger's buried story "Blue Melody," which the narrator protests is not a slam against the South or "anybody or anything," but
"just a simple little story of Mom's apple pie, ice-cold beer, the Brooklyn Dodgers, and [Cecil B. DeMille's] Lux Theater of the Air—the
things we fought for, in short."[14] Seymour Glass, like Holden Caulfield, was finally too earthbound—his flight was defiance, not acceptance; the model for what is identified in Salinger's next work as the
way of the pilgrim is Teddy McArdle, and he is not with us for very
long.

If many people did understand "Teddy," they almost certainly would
not like it. They are not willing to believe that there is no possibility
for spiritual fulfillment in the United States—especially when so many
inspiring television evangelists assure us that there is—or at least that
low-calorie beer and watching the televised antics of the (now Los An-
geles) Dodgers have not been worth fighting for. On the purely mundane level, however, "Teddy" is unsparingly satirical of the American

way of life—Teddy's upper middle-class parents and sister are obnoxious in every way; the scientists who has been investigating Teddy's powers are terrified of what they may discover; educator Nicholson, like Antolini in *Catcher in the Rye,* is a well-intentioned but bumbling busybody. For one as unworldly as Teddy, the only way is out of this world.

Nine Stories

Salinger's collection dramatizes a progressive series of alternatives to the problem of remaining spiritually *nice* in a *phony* world (Salinger's emphasis on "phoniness" probably develops in part from the Brahman concept of maya, which perceives the phenomenal world as illusory). From the Brahman viewpoint, the stories may be seen as a succession of vignettes of incarnations of the soul on its path from destructive self-indulgence to readiness for the long-desired union with the infinite.[15]

Salinger does not appear, however, to be proposing that we should all become Teddy McArdles. The point of the concluding story seems rather to be that those rare persons with Teddy's special gifts should be left like the artistically talented Sister Irmas to pursue their own destinies, without constant interference from the insensitive and meddlesome.

Some alternatives are rejected. The characters in "Pretty Mouth and Green My Eyes" are beyond redemption, like *The Damned* in Luchino Visconti's film, indicating Salinger's special horror of sexual promiscuity; and Teddy's parents and sister are still barbarians to be condemned—like many of those Holden meets in *Catcher in the Rye*—for their thoughtless presumptuousness. The outlook is bleak for the characters in "Uncle Wiggily in Connecticut," "Just before the War with the Eskimos," and "The Laughing Man," who are not strong enough to break through their physical handicaps or inhibiting illusions. "Down at the Dinghy" shows that there are some manifestations of evil that idealists like Salinger simply cannot deal with at all.

There remain Esmé and De Daumier-Smith as potential role models for achieving compassion through an acquaintance with squalor (though never on the level that Visconti, for example, presents it). The curious feature about these characters, however, who are making satisfactory spiritual progress without wishing to follow the impatient Seymour or the passive Teddy out of this world, is that they are the only two principal characters in Salinger's fiction who have grown up outside the United States in aristocratic environments. (It certainly does not seem coincidental that their stories were the two chosen by the London *World Review*.) The difference between these two stories of worldly success and all Salinger's others makes especially intriguing the question of why he himself never tried expatriation, as some of his contemporaries like Richard Wright, Paul Bowles, and the mysterious William Wharton did. Indeed we never again encounter characters like Esmé and De Daumier-Smith in his work. He chose instead to concentrate on the chronicles of the Glass Family, and as John Updike has most memorably said, "Their invention has become a hermitage for him."[16]

Chapter Five
The House of Glass

With "Teddy" Salinger had written himself into a cul-de-sac, for there was no obvious place to proceed from a hero (or *anti-hero* to use a then very fashionable term) who chose to fly this sphere of sorrows to end a cycle of earthly reincarnations in the long-sought final union with Brahma. It is also quite possible that Salinger felt that in his controversial story about the liberation of Teddy McArdle, he had pushed too far beyond his readers' susceptibilities during a period where he still felt concerned about them. Most Americans, even in the dreary 1950s, had not reached a state where they thought that the best way to deal with the world's problems was simply to leave them behind altogether.

The problem of finding a new direction must have preoccupied him for some time, because it was two years after the publication of *Nine Stories* in 1953, before his next story appeared in the *New Yorker,* although he had previously published at least one story every year, even during his service in the army, since his first contribution to *Story* in 1940. In the meantime, he had moved from fashionable Connecticut to the lonely woods of Cornish, New Hampshire, and had met Claire Douglas, whom he married in February 1955, only a few weeks after the publication of the first of a new sequence of five more stories, which appeared at increasingly long intervals over the decade until he ceased publishing.

"Franny"

Salinger did not settle on this final direction for his story-telling at once. Readers could find no indication that "Franny," which appeared in the *New Yorker* of 29 January 1955, had any relationship to the two earlier stories, "A Perfect Day for Bananafish" and "Down at the Dinghy," which featured members of the Glass family. Rather readers were somewhat scandalized to find that Salinger had left innocent children behind and was apparently writing about a distraught college girl who was experiencing a bout of morning sickness while visiting during a football weekend at an Ivy League college the arrogant boyfriend who was the father of her unborn child.

Almost two and one-half years passed before the title character of this earlier story was identified as Franny Glass, the youngest of Seymour's six siblings. It was also made clear that this Franny Glass was not pregnant during the morning episode with the boyfriend, but was, as sympathetic readers had thought all along, suffering a nervous breakdown resulting from a spiritual crisis.

But had the girl in the earlier story always been Franny Glass? Her last name was never mentioned in the story; some brothers were mentioned as having come to see her in a play, but they were not named. Franny Glass had appeared in November 1955 in "Raise High the Roof Beam, Carpenters," but she was not specifically identified as the girl from the earlier story, though readers probably took for granted that she was, because she would have been about the right age (Franny Glass is identified as eight in May 1942 in "Raise High the Roof Beam, Carpenters"). When "Zooey" in 1957 continued the story of "Franny" as that of Franny Glass, readers just assumed that this was what Salinger had had in mind all along.

John Updike cast doubts upon this easy assumption when he reviewed *Franny and Zooey,* the volume into which the two stories were collected in 1961, for the *New York Times Book Review,* but enthusiasts were too excited to pay attention to cavilers; during the first months after publication they made it Salinger's best-selling book.

Updike flatly asserts that the two Frannies were not the same girl. The first he describes as "a pretty college girl passing through a plausible moment of disgust," who comes from a family of "standard upper-middle class gentry" in "what is recognizably our world."[1] The second he describes as one of the "dream world" children of the vaudeville team of Gallagher and Glass. Updike seizes on a key discrepancy that Salinger tried rather clumsily to cover up in the second story. In "Franny," the title character borrows a book called *The Way of a Pilgrim* from the college library on the recommendation of the professor from whom she is taking a religion survey.[2] In "Zooey," her brother identifies the book she is carrying to their mother as *The Pilgrim Continues His Way,* a sequel to the other, both of which Franny got from Seymour's old room where they had been sitting on his desk for as long as Zooey can remember. Salinger does have mother Bessie Glass explain that boyfriend Lane Coutell had said that Franny got it from the college library, and it is plausible that Franny might not have wanted to reveal its actual source to the skeptical Lane. Updike is on quite firm ground when he wonders, however, "how a girl raised in a home where Buddhism and crisis theology were table talk could have postponed her own crisis so long, and, when it came, be so disarmed by it." Eberhard Alsen also questions whether a girl who had "received religious training in Seymour's 'home seminars' for many years" would have taken an introductory religion course in college.[3] Certainly the girl in the first story does not sound like a hardened veteran of the radio quiz program, "It's a Wise Child," on which sister Boo Boo reports that at eight she could stand her ground against an obtuse announcer ("Raise High the Roof Beam, Carpenters" [10]).

I do not agree with Alsen, however, that the story was written before "Teddy." Salinger's former wife Claire's brother has said that she was "hung on the Jesus Prayer," and Salinger did not meet her until after "Teddy" was published.[4] It seems entirely plausible that Salinger had seized upon the idea of a college girl's spiritual crisis as the basis for a contrasting companion piece to "Teddy" in a new series of stories about the difficulties of living a spiritual life in an egotistic society. In contrast to Teddy, whose spiritual quest ended in his departing this world, Franny becomes a pilgrim, humbly trying to preserve by praying without ceasing her spiritual integrity in spite of the obstacles posed by her supercilious and self-promoting boy friend, who disappears after a few frantic phone calls in "Zooey." Franny (whoever she may be) and Lane Coutell serve as excellent allegorical representations of the sacred and profane unhappily coupled. In any event, the story launched Salinger on a new cycle, one that resembled French filmmaker Eric Rohmer's later sequence of moral fables, including *My Night at Maud's* and *Claire's Knee,* although one wonders, as Updike also did, what even the original Franny and Lane could have seen in each other.

Read as the isolated story it may originally have been, "Franny" today does not stand up very well. Most readers have probably come to regard it as a necessary prologue to "Zooey," which carries us deeply into the history of the Glass family and Salinger's theories of artistic integrity. By itself, the story strains credibility. The leering and self-congratulating Lane is too much a caricature of the "section man" at an Ivy League college; he seems to have been too spitefully prompted to suggest compassionate detachment on the author's part. Franny, on the other hand, is just too much of a nervous wreck to have ever continued at one of the "seven sisters," even if she had survived the selection procedures of what now seems an undemanding time. It is easy to see why the first readers of the tale suspected Franny was pregnant; Lane is so insensitive to her condition and so intent on bedding her down, while her hysteria seems totally incommensurate to Lane's affectations that one cannot take it seriously unless Franny is truly "in trouble" in the sense intended in those days of curfews when *New Yorker* readers would have swooned at the thought of co-ed dormitories. (We need to be reminded today that in 1953 the use of the word *virgin* in Otto Preminger's lightweight comedy film *The Moon Is Blue* brought down thunderous condemnation from pulpits all over the nation.)

Properly attuned readers in those days, however, could share Franny's spiritual crisis. Salinger had a rich territory largely to himself. Eastern religious thought had, of course, attracted avant-garde Americans since the days of the transcendentalists in the nineteenth century, but the resolution of spiritual dilemmas that made Somerset Maugham's *The Razor's Edge* a best-seller in 1944 was still a somewhat suspect novelty even in trendy Manhattan. Enthusiasm for the swamis Salinger began to consult in the 1950s was just beginning to filter up from the underground (Allen Ginsberg's *Howl* was first delivered just a month before "Raise High the Roof Beam, Carpenters" appeared); and the Maharishi's mass marketing of transcendental meditation was almost a decade in the future, when it received a temporary assist from the Beatles.

New Yorker readers could share Franny's histrionic response to the dehumanizing ego, ego, ego of Madison Avenue's hollow men in gray flannel suits. Since then, however, readers have taken the road to minimalism after surviving the fragmentation of the meditation movement, the airport encounters with agents of the Hare Krishna, the rise and fall of the Bhagwam, the wedding of spirituality with high finance by Dr. Moon, and the campaigns of the native "Jesusfreaks" and television evangelists, with their "cash for God's sake" appeals, climaxing in the self-consuming holocaust at Jonestown. Lane's diffident skepticism and Franny's angst are less heart-rending today than when Salinger's "amateur readers" (see the dedication to his last book) were dazedly emerging from the convulsive dying days of McCarthyism.

Allen Ginsberg's *Howl* remains a much more powerful battlecry from a generation that had seen its "best minds destroyed" than Franny's vaporizings, and Lane's arch posturings now seem a trivial threat to humanism compared to the secret activities that we know now were then under way at our major universities. The road to the Orient—whether taken for our disastrous military adventure or a search for sentimental spirituality—has not proved a rewarding one for American pilgrims. "Franny" is today, much more than *Catcher in the Rye* or most of Salinger's nine stories, a period piece, reminding us of a time when perhaps the ultimate American failure resulted from an attempt to confront too much insensibility with too much sensibility.

"Zooey"

The critic now faces the problem of which path to follow through the few remaining works Salinger has shared with the public. Curiously, despite the striking disproportion between the amount of fiction that he has published and the critical commentary it has engendered, which led George Steiner even in 1959 before the 1963 peak to speak slightingly of a "Salinger industry," few monographs about limited aspects of his work have appeared. Eberhart Alsen's *Salinger's Glass Stories as a Composite Novel* (1983) stands alone as an effort to present "A Perfect Day for Bananafish" and the last five pieces that Salinger published in the *New Yorker* as constituting some form of larger whole like Jack Kerouac's projected "Duluoz Legend."

Alsen, in fact, finds the narrative possibly constituting parts of two uncompleted chronicles. His thesis is that "the thematic relationships among the six major stories suggest two obvious sequences in which to read them. One is the order in which they were published, which is also the order in which Buddy claims to have written them; and the other is the order suggested by the chronology of the events in the stories. Arranged one way, the stories focus on Buddy's struggle to understand Seymour by writing about him; arranged the other way, they focus on Seymour's quest for God."[5]

Following the second order produces an unfinished history of the family. Salinger announced in one of his rare statements about his intentions, on the dust jacket of his last published book, that he had "several new Glass family stories coming along," but only "Hapworth 16, 1924" has appeared in the quarter century since. Alsen fleshes out this episodic history with useful chapters on the roots of the family philosophy, particularly in Eastern religions and most particularly in

Advaita Vedanta, and a summary of what has been disclosed of Seymour's teachings. Alsen's detailed study provides a full discussion of the complexities of these subjects, which would be misrepresented by summary.

The pursuit of a coherent history of the family through these fragments, however, is finally artistically dissatisfying because of the discrepancies in dates and characterization that remain unresolved and the gaping holes in the account (we never learn, for example, how brother Waker happened to become a priest). Again one is struck by the resemblance to Jack Kerouac's "Duluoz Legend," although Kerouac did have plans to rework his stories into a coordinated whole, which he did not live to carry out.

The other approach to the Glass family stories also presents problems because Salinger appears to have been less concerned with the continually expanding role of Buddy as narrator than with finding—which he never did the published stories—a concept through which he, like Kerouac, could transform his own life into a legend, thus providing an adequate framework for a sequence of stories. In its present form, which Alsen thinks can in one sense can be regarded as complete, it is most nearly a modernist hagiography, the account of the life and martyrdom of a churchless saint.

The question that Alsen's theories pose, however, is whether at this point in a review of Salinger's career, one should proceed to follow a strictly chronological plan, which would necessitate turning now to "Raise High the Roof Beam, Carpenters," the first story to be published after "Franny" and the first to introduce all the members of the Glass family—however briefly some of them are dealt with; or whether one should leap ahead to "Zooey," which continues the account of the specific events introduced in "Franny." In the present state of what Alsen calls the "composite novel," it seems necessary to follow the second course, because there is in the final four published stories still another order to be considered beyond the two Alsen explains—one determined by what can best be called "the presence of Seymour." In "Zooey," his name is evoked, especially when Franny wants to talk to him, but he is not present, even through the departed spirit has left screeds behind. In "Raise High the Roof Beam, Carpenters," he is never physically present, but we read what he has written in his diary. In "Seymour: An Introduction," we are appropriately offered a much wider range of examples of what he actually said and wrote (though his poems are only paraphrased); then in "Hapworth 16, 1924," we are turned over into his hands completely to share an unedited letter. Since he was only seven when he wrote this, it must be regarded as one of his earliest efforts. It would seem that once Salinger had assumed Seymour's own voice, he would have planned to unveil his consecutively more mature statements, but we shall probably never be able to confirm this surmise. The most meaningful order in which to approach the last three stories to be collected, however, appears to be in the order in which they were published in books.

Although "Zooey" picks up Franny's story immediately after she has returned home from the dismal weekend with Lane, it is a much different kind of composition. "Franny" is a conventional third-person short story of a modern type with an ending that really resolves nothing—a kind of slice of fashionable upper middle-class life, particularly cultivated by John Cheever, for which the *New Yorker* was famous. "Zooey" is a far longer work, closest to the manner of a play-novelette like *The Moon Is Down,* which John Steinbeck had been experimenting with. It contains a group of scenes with extended conversations that could be transferred almost directly from the printed page to the stage; Salinger has the narrator Buddy Glass describe it as not "really a short story at all but a sort of prose home movie" (47).

Actually this analogy is not a very good one, for this production, which contains much talk and little action, hardly resembles most specimens of the cinema's contribution to the folk arts, which are usually characterized by frenetic action and little intelligent or intelligible dialogue. Kerouac comes far closer to achieving a convincing parallel in the "bookmovie" that is the second section of *Doctor Sax* (1959, but written in 1952).[6]

"Zooey" does resemble, however, the kind of motion picture that reached the screen decades after this story appeared, making Salinger's piece a more avant-garde work than he suggested. Its cinematic counterpart is not, however, the work of an amateur but the extremely sophisticated experiment of the daringly imaginative French filmmaker, Louis Malle, *My Dinner with André* (1982), which had the same kind of mixed reaction as Salinger's story, traditionalist critics finding both of them almost unbearably tedious. What is noteworthy about this entirely coincidental relationship, however, is that when Salinger attempted something that he described as folksy, the result was another example of sophisticated decadence. He might take to the hills, but he could not cast off his overcivilized background, a characteristic his analysts (literary and psychological) need to bear in mind.

To whatever subgenre "Zooey" might be assigned, it is terribly hard to take when the market for cinema-verité soul searching has been overexploited. Can anyone pick up this morality play today and plow through it with enthusiasm generated by the title character's harangues?

I wonder, in fact, if anyone ever could have if the story had not been signed by J. D. Salinger at a time of almost hysterical curiosity about the reclusive author and his fabulous creations. Updike was skeptical at the time the book version was published, commenting that "a lecturer has usurped the writing stand."[7] The disproportion between the substance of the story and its length (Kerry McSweeney counts forty-four thousand words) might even provoke the unlikely suspicion that Salinger was being paid by the word.[8] As Alsen points out, though with far greater enthusiasm than many other readers, the whole three-act conversion drama is a gloss on Christ's brief statement "Inasmuch as ye have done it unto of the least of these my brethren, ye have done it unto me" (Matt. 25:40).[9]

To return to the comparison with *My Dinner with André,* "Zooey" might work cinematically, since the interminable stage directions would be absorbed into the mise-en-scène of the Glass's cluttered apartment, and a roving camera could enable the eye to come to the relief of the overworked ear. The necessary overvoiced reading of Buddy's letter and the rendition of Zooey's playing Buddy over the telephone would also provide a unique challenge for even as inventive a talent as Louis Malle.

Why is such a vast superstructure necessary to lead to the restatement of one of the fundamental principles of Christianity in the therapeutic revelation that the kingdom of heaven is inside one and that "there isn't anyone *any*where who isn't Seymour's Fat Lady," who is really "Christ himself, buddy" (200)? Salinger may have belabored the point because he had been misunderstood before in *Catcher* and "Teddy" and "Franny." But in "Zooey" his concern seems excessive.

In "Raise High the Roof Beam, Carpenters," Seymour writes in his diary of taking Muriel to see an unidentified MGM film that is unquestionably William Wyler's *Mrs. Miniver.* (Incidentally, Seymour could not actually have taken Muriel to see this black-and-white World War II classic before their marriage; one wonders whether Salinger knew that ironically the film had its world premiere at the Radio City

Music Hall on 4 June 1942, the very day of the marriage.) Seymour observes that when a kitten is introduced into this saga of wartime sacrifice and spirit, "M. loved the kitten and wanted me to love it"; he responds chillingly with R. H. Blyth's definition of "sentimentality" as "giving a thing more tenderness than God gives to it" (78). Updike points out, however, that in "Zooey," Salinger himself is guilty of the very fault that Seymour criticizes in Muriel, because he "loves the Glasses more than God loves them. He loves them too exclusively."[10]

Twenty-five years ago, assessing Salinger's work, I wrote that "the longer I contemplate *Franny and Zooey,* the more certain I feel that the public has been right in its enthusiastic reception of the book's general 'message' about the advisability of improving one's self rather than criticizing others and that the reviewers have been right in their reservations about the craftsmanship of the presentation."[11]

During the quarter century between these two studies, no novel has come along that has replaced *The Catcher in the Rye* as a portrayal of the trauma of coming of age in upper middle-class urban America. I think, however, that *Franny and Zooey* has not only dated more rapidly than *Catcher,* but also that it has been superseded as the most affecting portrayal of its particular Upper East Side Manhattan apartment society by the films of Woody Allen, beginning with *Annie Hall* and including especially *Interiors, Manhattan,* and *Hannah and Her Sisters,* in which he abandoned the one-line jokes of his earlier farces for sustained portrayals of people with basically good intentions who are caught in situations that try the soul. Allen's characters in these films come from the same social and ethnic backgrounds as Salinger's and face similar crises. Allen himself shows the same suspicion of celebrity that Salinger does, and he has managed in the tough business of film, which is controlled by international financiers, to maintain an unusual degree of control over his works (he has even insisted that videocassette prints of his recent films be shown in their theatrical ratios and not be clipped for the narrow screen; but he does allow videocassettes to be circulated).

In a notoriously insensitive business, Allen has demonstrated that it remains possible for an American to maintain his independence and integrity and also to protect his privacy without abandoning Manhattan. As a result of his dedication and self-discipline, he has been able to give us through his films an authentic picture of the neuroses of mature members of one of the most influential societies in the world.

(Allen's picture of childhood in New York in *Annie Hall* and *Radio Days,* however, has nothing like the power of Salinger's novel.)

The point of this comparison is not just that Woody Allen has moved beyond Salinger in deepening the portrayal of this style-setting society, but even more that it was not essential for an artist of Salinger's stature to retire from the city to avoid the spotlight. Nor is this observation any criticism of Salinger's preference; it is meant only to suggest that a need for privacy alone is not enough to account for his rejection of his former life-style. His taking to the woods was a move toward, not just away from something. We cannot be surprised if his writings beginning with "Zooey" should carry him steadily further out of the workaday world.

Chapter Six
The Search for the Seer

Before Salinger published "Zooey" he had for undisclosed reasons resurrected Seymour Glass and composed an account of his wedding day
in 1942 as experienced by his younger brother Buddy, who in "Raise
High the Roof Beam, Carpenters" assumes the role of the keeper of the
sacred flame of his brother's memory. In this story Salinger also has
Buddy digress from the business principally before him to indulge in
"that David Copperfield kind of crap" about the Glass family, providing the background for further tales of its supernal brilliance, especially
the marathon participation of the seven siblings in the "It's a Wise
Child" radio quiz program. Salinger had apparently, however, not yet
worked out all the details of this history, for nowhere in this 1955
story is it mentioned that Buddy has become writer-in-residence at a
women's college in upstate New York.

Back in the days when Salinger allowed such things to happen, the
editors of the *New Yorker* selected "Raise High the Roof Beam, Carpenters" as Salinger's representative in their selection of stories that
graced the magazine between 1950 and 1960. Although he had published six other stories during his most active decade, including the
favorite of most anthologists, "For Esmé—with Love and Squalor," the
editors' choice is the appropriate one. The story marks the beginning
of the final and most spectacular phase of the author's relatively brief
and controversial publishing career; it is the first story to deal with the
Glass family rather than simply individual members of it in other con-
texts. More than that, Updike appears justified when he argues that
"Raise High the Roof Beam, Carpenters" is also the best of the Glass
family stories, "a magic and hilarious prose-poem with an enchanting
end effect of mysterious clarity."[1] Salinger's last three publications did
not elicit such praise because the magician had been replaced by the
lecturer.

The reappearance of Seymour Glass, whose legend had seemed fin-
ished with his suicide in the earliest of his stories that Salinger allowed
to be collected, "A Perfect Day for Bananafish," came as a surprise to

readers awaiting possibly more news of Franny, who also to their surprise was apparently one of Seymour's siblings. "A Perfect Day for Bananafish" had launched a cycle of stories about spiritual progress or the want of it that had apparently reached a dead end with "Teddy." Salinger returned to it for his final group of stories. Before turning to these, however, we need to flash backward to their progenitor.

Another Look at "Bananafish"

Readers have not needed critics to learn that there are discrepancies between the Seymour Glass who kills himself in "A Perfect Day for Bananafish" and the resurrected figure who haunts Salinger's last published works. There is even an unreconciled difference in the time of their deaths. "Bananafish" appeared in the *New Yorker* of 31 January 1948. The story ends with Seymour's shooting himself, but in "Zooey," Buddy Glass comments in a letter to his brother that the day he is writing, 18 March 1951, is "three years, to the day, since Seymour killed himself" (62), while in "Seymour: An Introduction," he also explains that the story was written "a couple of months after Seymour's death" (131), and not very long after Buddy returned from the European theater in World War II. Buddy is not likely to have forgotten such a traumatic day, but he may have forgotten the year that Salinger signed the story and sold it to the *New Yorker* for him. Most people had returned from Europe, where World War II ended in 1945, long before 1947. (Muriel also mentions in "Bananafish" visiting Florida as Seymour's wife before the war, although in "Carpenters," she and Seymour are married during the war.)

But Salinger is creating myth not writing history. Much more important to an understanding of the stories and the relationship between them is Buddy's belated explanation in "Seymour: An Introduction" that the "Seymour" in the "early story was not Seymour at all but, oddly, someone with a striking resemblance to—alley oop, I'm afraid—myself" (131). By thus freeing himself to recharacterize Seymour, Buddy/Salinger leaves as the only significant feature of the original story the shooting itself. We cannot even be certain that Seymour as finally introduced was even a "Capricorn," as he tells little Sybil in "Bananafish." Capricorn is Salinger's own sign; if Buddy has taken over his creator's history as well as his works, it could be his. Astrologists are going to have a rough time shedding much light on Saint Seymour. Rather than explaining anything about the enigmatic "Perfect Day for

Bananafish," the later stories shed doubt upon its authenticity as part of the kind of composite novel Eberhard Alsen builds from the stories. We are never enlightened about what happened to "all those lovely pictures from Bermuda." "A Perfect Day for Bananafish" is most satisfactorily regarded as an independent story within the context of *Nine Stories*.

"Raise High the Roof Beam, Carpenters"

We shall probably never know just what sent Salinger back to the character of Seymour Glass for his next story after "Franny," but the rest of the stories he has published make clear why he resurrected Seymour. He intended to turn him into a god-seeking seer, and the stories were intended to try to cajole the reader into accepting his evaluation of Seymour as he funnels it through the seer's devoted Boswell, his brother Buddy.

Seymour, however, has committed suicide, an action that is generally in the Judeo-Christian tradition branded a mortal sin. Salinger's problem thus became that of justifying Seymour's action so that the reader might love him as his creator does. He sought to do this by establishing Buddy Glass—as his nickname suggests—as a "buddy" to the reader, a process that begins by his prefacing "Raise High" with the Taoist tale of a judger of horses to enable Buddy to put across his point that since his brother's "permanent retirement from the scene," he cannot think of anyone he would "care to send out to look for horses in his stead" (6). As Alsen points out, the story also "relies heavily on a new narrative element that is to become a hallmark of Buddy's later fiction, of quotations from religious writings, from letters, from memoirs, and from diaries."[2]

Alsen creates unnecessary difficulties for himself, however, when he tries to treat "Raise High" as a more conventional short story than it is in order to stress Buddy's increasing eccentricities in "Zooey" and "Seymour: An Introduction." He bogs down in a finally pointless discussion of *whom* the story is about that resembles many of the idle speculations on whether Fitzgerald's *The Great Gatsby* is about Gatsby or narrator Nick Carraway when the seemingly obvious point is that the story is about the influence on Nick of his piecing together the story of Gatsby's doomed "grail quest." It is *about* Nick's writing about Gatsby. "Raise High" is much more indebted to *Gatsby* than has been recognized. (It is hardly surprising that Fitzgerald's novel exercised such an influence, for Buddy confides in "Zooey" that it was his *Tom Sawyer* when he was twelve [49]).

While, as Alsen observes, Seymour does not appear in "Raise High," he dominates the latter part of the story through his diary entries. In fact, Seymour dominates this story even more than Gatsby does his because Buddy Glass is a comparatively transparent medium. We never learn what influence his discoveries about Seymour's doomed love for Muriel (who like Daisy Buchanan has a voice "full of money") has on his actions. Alsen's insistence on trying to make the story Buddy's history rather than just his chronicle leads him into a misconstruction that raises some questions about his whole interpretation of the family saga.

After explaining how Seymour's diary entries lead Buddy to an understanding of Seymour's affection for Muriel, Alsen makes the sound judgment that Seymour needs "Muriel's simplicity and undiscriminating heart just as Muriel needs his intellectual and spiritual values." But he follows with this: "Thus, on its most basic level of meaning, 'Raise High the Roof Beam, Carpenters,' makes a statement about the relationship between intellectuals like the Glasses and normal people like the Fedders. This statement concerns two related problems, the alienation of the intellectuals and the anti-intellectualism of the average middle-class Americans. Unlike other works in American literature that deal with this theme, 'Carpenters' blames the intellectuals and not the middle-class Americans for these problems" (42). One does a double take and backs up to reassure oneself that he has called the Fedders "normal"; but, yes, he is succumbing to the tendency of American intellectuals to feel guilty about being intellectuals and to pay penance by feigning a sympathy for all sorts of kitsch. "Typical" the Fedders indeed are, but not "average" in income or status and "normal" only if one concedes that bad taste and lack of intellectual curiosity constitute a desirable standard to be perpetuated, as one might speak of actual physical starvation being "normal" in parts of the Third World. Of course American intellectuals have had dungforkfuls of guilt heaped on them because of past economic and political naïveté; but if intellectuals (and people who write perceptive literary criticism are intellectuals no matter how much it may embarrass their in-laws) take on the defense of the very middle-class vulgarity that Holden Caulfield rails against, it is small wonder that nervous people like Salinger take to the woods.

"Raise High the Roof Beam, Carpenters" does not blame intellectuals for refusing to kowtow to vulgarly materialistic antiintellectual-ism. The victor in the struggle that unfolds through the story is, at least temporarily, Seymour. He does not give in to Mrs. Fedder's half-baked psychoanalytic busybodying or her pretentious obeisance to so-cial-climbing rituals. He not only triumphs over people like the bul-lying matron of "honor" and her castrated officer husband; but he succeeds in spiriting Muriel away from the trappings of the "non-denominational" wedding and ostentatious show-of-wealth reception. She does indeed need his "intellectual and spiritual values," and in this story seems to be on the road to grasping something of them.

This joyful epithalamium records the high point of their triumph over the incipient fascism of American antiintellectualism. What ul-timately defeats these promising expectations is Seymour's long ab-sence fighting a desensitizing war and his institutional confinement in a military hospital, while the long years at home, still unboxing her mother's Christmas ornaments, must have overwhelmed Muriel's spirit as Walt's death did Eloise's in "Uncle Wiggily in Connecticut."

A clue to what has happened to Muriel during Seymour's absence is found in "A Perfect Day for Bananafish" (although the tough Muriel there is Buddy's conception, not the too malleable figure in Seymour's diary entries in "Raise High"). We meet her reading an article entitled "Sex Is Fun—or Hell" in one of the *Reader's Digest*ish magazines that abound on American newsstands. The title reflects the typical antiin-tellectual presumption that these polar opposites are the only alterna-tives; but the view that emerges from Salinger's stories is that sex, while it frequently is fun or hell, need not and should not be either; it should rather be a sacred religious ritual. The real message of "Raise High the Roof Beam, Carpenters" is found in Seymour's last premarital diary entry about his miscellaneous readings in the Vedanta: "Marriage partners are to serve each other. Elevate, help, teach, strengthen each other, but above all, *serve*," a message that is reinforced by the tribute to marriage that Boo Boo Glass has inscribed on the bathroom mirror and that provides the title for the story (106, 76).

"Raise High the Roof Beam, Carpenters" is neither so much about either Seymour or Buddy, as it is Salinger's effort to persuade the reader to share his assessment of Seymour. To draw a parallel from modern art criticism, Salinger's Buddy Glass narratives are highly experimental works because they are not so much representational as presentational, that is, they are not intended to serve as "mirrors in the roadway," reflecting an action ("mimetic" as *The Catcher in the Rye* is), but rather to give communicable form to a vision, so as to be best called "mythical." Salinger's awareness of modern art criticism sometimes shyly surfaces, as in a passage in "Seymour: An Introduction" about using "some sort of literary Cubism to present his face," although Buddy's instincts are "to put up a good, lower-middle-class fight against it" (199).

Again the influence of *The Great Gatsby* can be seen if the stories about Seymour beginning with "Raise High the Roof Beam, Carpenters" are perceived not as a godlike author's manipulation of puppets, but as the diary of an author himself in quest of a grail.

Because Alsen takes an approach to the work that is too prosaic, he is puzzled as to whether Buddy achieves an understanding of Seymour's feelings about Muriel on the day of their wedding or only years later when he is writing the account of the day. As usual, however, Salinger sprinkles clues that limit readers' options for interpreting events. Perhaps the cardinal principle to remember in dealing with the writings that Salinger has chosen to keep in print is that he is in charge. If Buddy had not grasped the message of Seymour's diary as he read it on the wedding day, he would not have been able to drop off into the sleep that would allow him, like his doppelgänger Sergeant X in "For Esmé," to keep his faculties intact.

Alsen obscures that which Buddy discovered on the day of Seymour's wedding by failing to reconcile his accounts of one of the most crucial episodes in Seymour's history in his development of the account of the two ways in which the stories might be read as a composite novel. In the diary quoted in "Raise High the Roof Beam, Carpenters," Seymour refers to the time when he was nine years old and threw a rock at the faultlessly beautiful (but dumb) Charlotte Mayhew, slightly disfiguring her face permanently; but Salinger dodges the issue of having to come up with a full explanation here by having Seymour state that he had no intention of discussing the incident with a psychiatrist over only one drink. Thus, Salinger can assign the last word on this crucial matter to his alter ego Buddy.

Subsequently Buddy, who has been reading the diary, has also discovered on the day of the wedding that Muriel (whom he had not yet met) is the spitting image of Charlotte. After this, he discloses to the matron of honor, who has been maligning Seymour's behavior, that Seymour threw the rock at Charlotte "because she looked so beautiful sitting there in the middle of the driveway with Boo Boo's cat" (104).

Buddy then tells the company that everyone present at the incident, including Charlotte, understood this, but then confesses in an aside to the reader that Charlotte never did understand. The reader, however, may still be at a loss to understand why someone should deliberately try to disfigure someone beautiful, as this sounds like the psychotic behavior of vandals who try to deface famous paintings—hardly behavior that would encourage one to venerate Seymour. In his explanation of Seymour's spiritual growth, Alsen comes up with what appears to be the explanation that gives the rock-throwing incident its proper significance in Seymour's history when he explains that "when Seymour threw the stone at Charlotte, he threw it at the person who he thought would make him relinquish the paths of study and meditation" (189). He was resisting the temptation of the flesh—an effort that he was subsequently going to have to give up altogether when he met Charlotte's look-alike, Muriel. When Muriel then subsequently fails to live up to his expectations of a spouse, he realizes the futility of continuing a life that promises no further spiritual development.

The incident of throwing the rock at Charlotte is the early key to understanding Seymour's vision and his doom; but it has to be approached consistently in any theories about the linking of the Glass family stories. It also requires emphasis because many readers are going to have great difficulty even comprehending the idea of the necessity of rejecting the appeal of material beauty in order to make spiritual progress, and many, of course, are not going to accept it even after it is explained.

The episode helps clarify Buddy/Salinger's meaning when he provides the key explanation in "Seymour: An Introduction" of the reasons for the suicide of "the true artist-seer"—as he considers Seymour: "the heavenly fool who can and does produce beauty, is mainly dazzled to death by his own scruples, the blinding shapes and colors of his own sacred human conscience" (123). These scruples necessitate his throwing the rock that disfigures Charlotte to try to overcome the early stirrings of his sexuality, which we learn in "Hapworth 16, 1924" displayed the same kind of precocity as his intellectual development. But the very necessity of such violence foreshadows his inevitable fate, for his lustful instincts preclude the spiritual development for which he longs. He simply is not that close to his desired goal of the Vedantic concept of *mukti*—permanent liberation from the flesh. As we have seen in the analysis of the cycle of *Nine Stories,* Seymour's history resembles that of Teddy's previous incarnation.

"Raise High the Roof Beam, Carpenters" is, however, the lovingly told story of the moment that the god seeker seemed to have achieved a victory over the Fedders (fetters?) of this world. Considered from this viewpoint, the story works. It is a piece of master craftsmanship that deserves preservation. Salinger has hit upon the way to tell the story that he wants to tell and to do it without any reliance on traditional theories of narration, but with only a respectful tribute to the example of Scott Fitzgerald.[3]

Does it work, however, on the reader to the point that one accepts Buddy-Salinger's high opinion of Seymour as a judge of horses? This question can only be answered by the individual reader; and as just one of these, I can only say that in this respect, it has not worked on me. I admire the production, but I do not buy its message. Perhaps I am a hard sell, but many other critics seem also to have had misgivings about the author's line in this story and its companion pieces. I have enjoyed what I have earlier described as his even temporary victory over middle-class pretentiousness and bad taste, but it is clearly not such worldly victories he seeks.

The problem about Seymour arises when he begins to champion indiscrimination "on the ground that it leads to health and a kind of very real, enviable happiness" (86). Even he has misgivings, however, when he realizes that one would have to "dispossess himself of poetry," drop it completely, because "he couldn't possibly learn to drive himself to *like* bad poetry in the abstract, let alone equate it with good poetry" (86).

But why only poetry? Even if, for the sake of argument, we accept the idea of poetry as the supreme human achievement, how could one learn to like bad painting or bad music or bad food or a bad environment? As for going *beyond* poetry, this means again out of this world altogether. There is simply no way of surviving in a world in which the bad tends to drive out the good without making discriminations. John Updike is correct that the Glass stories take place in a dream world; they are escapist fantasies. Escapist fantasies have their place in human experience, but problems arise when we confuse them with maps of the possible. Seymour does not seem to have the qualities that one would expect to find in a judge of horses. It is small wonder that in subsequent revelations, Salinger, as Updike observed, in his demands that readers love his characters, begins to rob those readers "of the initiative upon which love must be given" (56).

"Seymour: An Introduction"

Salinger had not been heard from for more than two years when readers of the *New Yorker* for 6 June 1959, some no doubt already at their summer retreats not far from where Salinger had composed the piece, found much of the issue devoted to an introduction to a character that many had already met as long ago as eleven years before—Seymour Glass.

The long composition—neither the traditional term *story* or even *narrative* will serve here—proved to be Salinger's most original experiment in attempting to manipulate readers. Far from following the *New Yorker* tradition, however, of distancing performers from spectators with the cool impersonality of the glass and steel that pushes skyward in Manhattan, Salinger, an old hand now at sending messages from a green and unpolluted hinterland, was working out his own wily variations on the techniques of the medicine man peddling nostrums to the folks down home.

Although speaking through the ventriloquist's dummy Buddy Glass, Salinger, unless he was masterminding one of the most preposterous put-ons in literary history (some unkind judges have suspected this, but playing such a tricky game seems totally incompatible with the asperity of his early writings and the short fuse he has always exhibited in encounters with the public), was speaking for himself in his slashing attacks on many features of contemporary American life ("the middle-aged hot rodders who insist on zooming us to the moon, the Dharma Bums," etc.[114]) and wheedling hammock-readers into joining him in fashioning a saint for cynical times. It is in "Seymour: An Introduction" that, as fellow novelist Mary McCarthy observed, "the ordinary relation is reversed, and instead of the reader reading Salinger, Salinger, the Man of Sorrows, is reading the reader."[4]

After depressing introductory quotations from Kafka and Kierkegaard about writers' inability to do justice to their subjects, Salinger addresses himself to "the general reader as my last deeply contemporary confidant." But he questions how a writer can "observe the amenities if he has no idea what his general reader is like" (112). He proceeds to address this "general reader" as "you" and to distinguish himself and this "you" from "the grounded everywhere." Then follows ten pages of special pleading to these supersensitive persons who are attuned to the sufferings of artists like Kafka and Van Gogh and Seymour who have been made ill by their genius. All this leads to the statement about "the true artist-seer" being "dazzled to death by his own scruples."

One can either buy this pronouncement or shop elsewhere, but it is a potent appeal that the aficionado who has been following Salinger through a decade when scruples have commanded quite a premium rejects at the peril of being cast forever among the philistines. Salinger is clearing the site for a separation of sheep from goats, as Seymour's qualifications for designation as "true artist-seer" are set forth.

Once this "credo is stated" (123) ordinary academic criticism of the kind that Stephen Dedalus was taught to write in James Joyce's *A Portrait of the Artist as a Young Man* becomes beside the point. Salinger tries to forestall it by specifying that these "undetached prefatory remarks" have nothing to do with "the short-story form" (125). In dealing with Seymour, in any event, the important part of the compound describing him is not "artist" (we know of his poems only through paraphrases) but "seer." We are dealing with something not profane, but sacred, so that what is required is not criticism, but testimony. The fact that the beneficiary of the testimony is fictional is also beside the point because many venerated religious figures may also be fictional. What is required is not judgment but conversion. Salinger does show signs even in this next to last published story of becoming unnerved by the project he has undertaken. "How well do I know the reader? How much can I tell him without unnecessarily embarrassing either of us?" he asks some twenty-five thousand words along as the introduction nears its end (237). The response to the Glass family stories may have provided more discouraging answers than he would acknowledge. His ceasing publication may have been at bottom a failure of nerve. A writer cannot get hung up on such a question and remain in business.

The response has not been entirely negative. It is impossible to tell how many others, for example, Alsen speaks for, when he writes that "my attitude toward the Glass stories is not that of a detached critic but that of an undetached rhapsode" (xii). At the other extreme, the notably uncharitable Mary McCarthy might have been moved in discussing another best-selling novelist by spite or jealousy, but it must still have been discouraging to have found her announcing in *Harper's* that "Salinger's world contains nothing but Salinger."[5]

There is a middle ground. Even if "Seymour" is not a convincing work, it is a fascinating exercise. What Salinger is attempting to do is basically religious rather than artistic—he is trying to share a dream, as prophets who have succeeded and the many who have failed have always tried to do. Even if he does not succeed, it is illuminating to watch him make the effort to create a myth.

Eberhard Alsen provides a quite detailed account of a careful and subtle plan underlying the seeming formlessness of "Seymour"; much of any such account, however, is only a paraphrase of the work, and if one is going to contend with the work, it is better to read Salinger himself than any paraphrase. Stringing together quotations would serve no purpose even if it were permissible. Alsen puts his finger on exactly what needs to be said about "Seymour" when he observes that "what is particularly impressive about the 'Introduction' is the way in which its form expresses its meaning," a tribute to its success as a work of presentational art. Alsen is right also when he comments that "the 'Introduction' marks the high point of Buddy's development as a writer" (75). One does wish that Salinger had gone on experimenting with this presentational form in which the writer at least pretends to share with the reader the process of constructing the composition. What prompted him to make the disastrous shift to the method of his next story, "Hapworth 16, 1924"?

A clue may be that Salinger may have fallen into the very trap that Buddy talks about when, nearing the end of the long task he has set for himself in "Seymour," he describes it as possibly "a bad description," because his own ego, his "lust to share top billing with [Seymour], is all over the place" (248). Salinger may have become impatient with working through the medium of Buddy, although the use of this alter ego was probably the best idea he had had since he chose first-person narration as the medium for the final version of *The Catcher in the Rye*.

"Hapworth 16, 1924"

Buddy appears only briefly to introduce Salinger's last published story, which has only been printed once, in the *New Yorker* of 19 June 1965. He then steps back from the role of composer to that of transcriber, as Seymour himself takes over the pen—or in this case pencil.

"Hapworth 16, 1924" was a long time coming. Just slightly over six years had elapsed since the appearance of "Seymour: An Introduction," during which the four stories printed beginning in 1955 had been collected into two volumes in the early 1960s at the peak of "the Salinger industry." It obviously took Salinger a long time to decide how to follow up "Seymour"; but he appears not to have been satisfied with the choice he made, for "Hapworth" has never been reprinted.

Looking back over Salinger's work from a long perspective, however, we can see that he must have been moving toward taking on the Seymour persona himself for a long time, though he moved very cautiously, assigning only a few bits of conversation and diary entries directly to him. What would necessarily have been one of his earliest letters would seem an appropriate way to begin letting him speak for himself. Had Salinger ever planned to publish the poems that Buddy had been sitting on since 1948?

Any scrutinizing of "Hapworth" has to begin with the acknowledgment that in the course of this bold experiment something went wrong. We will probably never know all the reasons that Salinger began to find publication an invasion of his privacy, but one must certainly be that his long isolation from the public had gotten him out of touch with it. One of the qualities most often praised in Salinger's writing, especially *The Catcher in the Rye*, is the authenticity of his characters' language; but by 1965 it had been a long time since he had heard these voices. As happened to John Steinbeck when he left California for the East, he lost touch with the spoken language that inspirited his best prose. He became preachy. So did Salinger.

For about two-thirds of its length, the letter from camp that is the substance of "Hapworth" proceeds quite enjoyably if one can accept the initial premise that this masterly example of epistolary form is the spontaneous creation of a seven-year-old. Regarded as the product of a very bright, very bookish boy some years older, however, it becomes plausible as one of the most heart-rending evocations of an exquisitely sensitive young person trapped in a situation for which even he can find no physical or metaphysical justification, giving vent to what Buddy in "Seymour" calls one of those "cries of pain" to which people do not listen properly, concluding, "We send you our naked hearts."

Then in one of those monstrous mischances in the secret history of creativity, at a point where the letter should properly end and Seymour should wait to see if he evoked any response, he finds another pad of paper and takes off again, extending the letter almost half its length over in a pompous display of erudition that many commentators have found simply unreadable.

What happened appears to be a repetition of one the few episodes from Salinger's life that he has shared with the public through information he provided a fellow *New Yorker* writer William Maxwell back in the days before Salinger could hold out against the Book-of-the-Month Club. Aspiring writer Salinger had been invited to speak to a short story class at Sarah Lawrence College. While he enjoyed the day, he confessed, "It isn't something I'd ever want to do again. I got very oracular and literary. I found myself labeling all the writers I respect."[6] But he did it again. In the last third of "Hapworth," in the guise of child Seymour, Salinger turns both "oracular and literary." He does not just name writers, but comments on them, describing the Brontë sisters, for example, as "ravishing girls." Nor does he limit himself, as he had told Maxwell a writer should, to the writers that he loves. The approved reading list turns into a condemnatory review with a seven-year-old delivering a withering indictment of the motives behind the writings of two apparently fictitious contemporaries, Alfred Erdonna and Theo Acton Baum.

Salinger begins "discriminating" in this story in just the way Seymour had condemned the practice in "Raise High the Roof Beam, Carpenters." After allowing the story to be printed, Salinger must have recognized that he was again doing what he had said he never wanted to do again. It seems apparent that on the day at Sarah Lawrence, Salinger had simply gotten carried away by his own enthusiasm and the tensions that build up during such sessions and had lost the control of the situation that he always most prized. Now the same thing had happened in print. He had begun to go on in a way that might prove embarrassing. Such a development alone could have driven him to the decision—as the day at Sarah Lawrence did—to permit no such further invasions of his privacy.

Alsen has made the most detailed analysis of "Hapworth" (few others have had such sympathy or patience), since the story provides the climactic evidence for his treatment of the Glass family narratives as a composite novel. He proves that, like "Zooey" and "Seymour: An Introduction," the story is much more carefully structured than the rambling epistolary form at first suggests; there appears to be little purpose, however, in working through his arguments, for not that many readers seem interested in lingering long over a story they have found disappointing, and Alsen does not succeed in proving that "Hapworth," despite its artistry, is better than generally supposed.

Something does need to be said, however, about the "mode of address" employed by Seymour as letter writer, for the tone of his remarks to the intended recipients of the letter shows that Salinger still possessed a great skill in characterization. Unfortunately, to put matters bluntly, it was really wasted on the particular subject, since Seymour's comments do serve to provide most depressing evidence about the character of the fictional figure and of the forces that may have propelled the author in creating him.

Most of the limited criticism of "Hapworth" has focused on the supermannish aspects of Seymour—his sometimes clouded visions, his precocious reading tastes and sexuality, his psychoanalyzing of his elders (usually to exploit them to his own advantage), and especially his ability to cut the communication of pain from his wounded leg to his brain. Salinger is evoking Seymour as a shaman, a streetwise guru for his family, but also, through the preservation of his letter, potentially for the world.

Seymour is no simple reporter of facts. He is inordinately self-conscious (for one of any age) about the audience for his version of the first days at summer camp, which neither he nor Buddy wanted to attend. He spends much of his space telling the members of his family how they are to read the letter and obliquely punishing the parents for their progenies' exile.

The tenor of the whole seemingly endless message is set by the early sentence, "My God, let me achieve missing my beloved family without yearning that they quite miss me in return!" (It would be difficult indeed to express the quintessence of self-pitying sensibility in fewer words.) After this start, the mode of address is particularized for individual recipients.

Seymour assumes that his Jewish entertainer-father Les Glass (who remains a shadowy patriarchal figure in the whole saga) is not going to have any patience with Seymour's long-winded sob story and is going to disappear to the apartment house lobby for long periods while the golden-voiced mother is reading the letter aloud for the benefit of anyone within earshot. At times, Les is even condescendingly given Seymour's permission to leave the room, a defense mechanism of a brilliant and sensitive child who bitterly resents his father's lack of interest in him. In view of the invisibility of the fathers in most of Salinger's fiction, one gets the feeling that the artist's conviction is that, as in much American fiction, father-son relationships are not competitive, but simply nonexistent. Pa does not really want to hear about the kids' growing pains or else why would he ship them off to summer camp?

To Irish songstress-mother Bessie Gallagher Glass, who it is evident Seymour thinks will be the letter's most avid reader (she is the one who preserves it), Seymour's tone is also condescending, yet in a kinder but still astonishing, leprechaunish way. She is instructed about surgery she needs, about contemplating plans for retirement from the stage, even about the way she should sing a song to create a hit record. One of the most audacious features of the story is the way that this seven-year-old lectures an experienced vaudeville trouper on the conduct of her career. There are, of course, other such fictional brats, especially in some of the Shirley Temple films of the 1930s from which Seymour seems in part derived despite the sex change, but generally their intimidated parents are treated like comical boobs; there is no humor, however, in Salinger's portrayal of Seymour as child savant.

In the brief passages late in the letter directed to the younger siblings—the twin boys Walter and Waker and sister Beatrice (Boo Boo), the tone is not just pompous—as in the advice to their mother—but downright dogmatic. Seymour in the role of older brother is an authoritarian, not to be crossed or argued with, in the apparent lack of firm parental guidance in family crises. One increasingly wonders why this guiding light was not subsequently directed at a delinquent world. Again Salinger seems to have lacked the nerve to live up to his possibly embarrassing visions.

If Seymour's personality, as expressed most fully—despite his youth—in this letter, might be summed up in one word, it is *overbearing,* as confirmed by reports in earlier letters of his behavior on the "It's a Wise Child" radio show. In "Hapworth" we are back to the original Seymour of "A Perfect Day for Bananafish." He is, as argued in chapter 3, the kind of petulant child who demands constant attention from parents and playmates and who, if he does not get the attention he craves, devises constantly more conspicuous and dangerous ways to attract notice. He is condescending not only to parents and siblings, but also to the staff at Camp Hapworth, upon whom he uses even intimidation and threats of violence when his manipulative wiles do not achieve his purposes. These sorely beset hirelings no doubt wish just as much as the boys themselves that the Glass brothers had been kept at home.

Such a personality would scarcely have much appeal to readers seeking thoughtful fiction at any time, but Seymour appeared in his fullest manifestation at a particularly bad moment. The sixties generation was already in full rebellion when Salinger's fiction declined somewhat in popularity because of reaction against his generally passive characters by an increasingly activist intelligentsia.

Salinger's long hold on teenage readers was briefly threatened by the rise of the Beat Generation, beginning in 1955. Although Salinger has made few comments about contemporaries, his opening remarks in "Seymour: An Introduction" show his distaste for "Dharma Bums" and "the Beat and the Sloppy and the Petulant" (114). His attack on petulance is particularly eyebrow raising in view of the conduct of Seymour Glass and his brothers and even Holden Caulfield in his relationships with his schoolmates; but the principal emphasis in the sequence just quoted should fall on "sloppy" because Salinger has always exhibited a finicky eliteness that was one of the principal targets of the Beats.

They were, however, because of the enormous publicity that only too late they realized might destroy their influence, too vulgar to shake Salinger or his cultists; a more serious threat arose during the long period of silence between "Seymour: An Introduction" and "Hapworth," when the Beats gave way to the Beatles and their court of hippies, the flower people, first of the counterculture movements to show little interest in literature and none in the literary traditions of the past that the Beats had. Rock music and psychedelic posters became the preferred art form of the Haight-Ashbury set, which spread everywhere from San Francisco.

"Hapworth 16, 1924" emerged into a world where the only two recent American writers to win cult followings among the hippies, yippies, and their successors were Ken Kesey with *One Flew over the Cuckoo's Nest* (1962) and Richard Brautigan with *Trout Fishing in America,* written in 1961, but not published until 1967. (*A Confederate General from Big Sur* had appeared in 1964 to launch his underground reputation.)

Kesey and Salinger have a great deal in common, though it is not likely that Salinger would admit it. After an enormous success with their first novels, both became cult favorites of succeeding decades and, after their experiences with celebrity, both withdrew to the country to enjoy a retired pastoral life. Before his withdrawal, however, Kesey had established a much more spectacular rapport with his audience than Salinger could ever have countenanced, through his participation in light-shows and other adventures in psychedelia, especially through his cross-country bus trip in 1964 with the Merry Pranksters, which is chronicled in Tom Wolfe's *The Electric Kool-Aid Acid Test*; and he has kept in at least fitful touch with the public since his return to the farm.

Kesey has in *Cuckoo's Nest* protested against the same dehumanized urban society that upset Holden Caulfield; and his Patrick McMurphy resembles Seymour Glass in that each voluntarily gives up his life to escape an institutionalized world that he can no longer tolerate. The characters' motives are, however, diametrically opposed. McMurphy permits himself to be destroyed by authoritarians in the hope that his sacrifice may inspire and free others, as indeed it does Chief Bromden. Whatever Seymour's may be, they are basically self-indulgent, a petulant rejection of a world that he has found he cannot control, despite Salinger's calling these sentiments "scruples." Seymour is ironically more like Big Nurse in Kesey's novel than he is like the raffish McMurphy; he was, therefore, not likely to win the hearts of Kesey's audience, who to show their defiance of an establishment gone berserk burned draft cards and escaped to Canada instead of to Nirvana. They would also not have been likely to plow patiently through Seymour's reading list at the end of "Hapworth," let alone the inordinate number of books prescribed.

Alsen argues that "It may well be that Buddy did not publish any more stories after 'Hapworth' because he realized that his work no longer pleased and enlightened many readers" (109). Many other critics have not found this story—or even some of the preceding ones—pleasing or enlightening; and the principal reason appears to be that they do not find Salinger's Glass family dynamic enough.

At the end of "Seymour: An Introduction," as Buddy prepares for the sleep that marks the resolution of a crisis in Salinger's work, he observes in conclusion, "Seymour once said that all we do our whole lives is go from one little piece of Holy Ground to the next. Is he *never* wrong?" (248). Many people would agree with the underlying conception that all the earth should be sacred—a concept expressed with the greatest dignity in William Faulkner's "The Bear."

Seymour's sweeping overgeneralization, however, leaves the impression that all the earth remains the Garden of Eden if one but looks at it that way. Much of this holy ground, however, has been desecrated; and it is going to require work without ceasing to restore its sacredness. The problem here actually goes back to "Franny" and the injunction to "pray without ceasing" rather than to "work without ceasing" that pleases those who do not want to do anything themselves but hope that God will set things aright. Among the visionaries rarely mentioned in the Glass papers in William Blake, although many readers feel that the spiritual message projected through these papers might be strengthened and deepened if more heed were paid Blake's injunction not to "cease from Mental Fight," "till we have built Jerusalem in England's green and pleasant land" (or New England or wherever).

One cannot, of course, prescribe what Salinger should write; but one can defend what one chooses to read. If Alsen is right about Buddy/Salinger's discovery that his writings no longer pleased or enlightened readers, one can only praise his decision to continue to write for his own pleasure and leave him to his own devices.[7]

Chapter Seven

A "Nice and Peaceful" Place, Cornish

Perhaps the greatest irony of secretive Jerome David Salinger's life is that it has disproved a principal thesis of the novel on which his reputation remains most largely based. At the depth of his despair, just before the "fall" that redeems him, Holden Caulfield, demoralized by the obscenities he finds in what should be sacred places, laments, "You can't ever find a place that's nice and peaceful, because there isn't any" (*The Catcher in the Rye,* 264), and his story ends with his reluctant acceptance by "missing everybody" in the world as it is.

But Salinger himself discovered that there is "a nice and peaceful" place. His particular refuge is not, as Holden Caulfield fantasized from American popular myth, "Out West where it was very pretty and sunny" (257), but only a few hundred miles from dehumanizing Manhattan in the Upper Valley of the Connecticut River in New England, where it is very pretty and often foggy, in Cornish, New Hampshire.

Salinger has generally been successful at blocking out any glimpses into the life that he has led since the 1950s in what Hugh Mason Wade describes as a lofty "Tyrolean lodge" that the author has built on the "southern shoulder of Read's Hill"; but we can learn something of the natural charm and unique history of the remote community to which he has retreated.[1]

No one has disclosed just what brought Salinger to Cornish rather than to any of the other picturesque spots along the Connecticut. He might have found much greater isolation, for example, in the more forbidding terrain of Cavendish, Vermont, about thirty miles southwest, where the Russian emigré novelist Aleksandr Solzhenitsyn has sought refuge behind barbed-wired fences on his hillside estate; or he might have chosen the gentler hills just across the Connecticut, where movie tough guy Charles Bronson and his wife, Jill Ireland, evade intruders. Cornish had been a writer's and an artist's colony long before

Salinger's arrival, but it seems unlikely that this now-vanished society influenced his choice.

Cornish is almost out of this world. There are still only five roads into this thirty-six-square-mile division of Sullivan County, which reached its peak population in 1860. One of these—the only one from Vermont—is over the longest covered bridge still in use in the United States, the 1866 replacement for one originally erected in 1796, variously known as the Cornish-Windsor Bridge or the Windsor-Cornish Bridge, depending on which side of the stream you view the question from. The others are on State Roads 12-A or 120, which make their leisurely, winding ways along the river or eastern valley sides of the town, respectively. Both of these begin in Claremont, New Hampshire, and lead through Lebanon to Hanover, about twenty miles above Cornish where Dartmouth College is located. Salinger does not live near either, but in the northwestern part of the town, on a dirt road that is reached from the few paved highways by two other dirt roads, all of which may be snow covered for several months before the spring thaws turn them to mud.

When Salinger first came to Cornish, he lived across the road from his present residence in "a small salt-box house, . . . which had been built by the young architect John Dodge and his wife, Carlota, the granddaughter of Augustus Saint-Gaudens," the sculptor.[2] This early twentieth-century house went to Salinger's wife in the divorce settlement.[3] (She has not, however, remained in the area.) He now enjoys a splendid view from his hilltop over the Saint-Gaudens National Historic Site, the only national landmark of this type in New England, and across the Connecticut River and the old bridge, to charming Windsor, Vermont, the original state capital, and nearby Mount Ascutney, a lonely eminence detached from any range that resembles those in Japanese woodblock prints. He is not the first to find this serene setting his Shangri-La.

Cornish, named for its patentee, the Duke of Cornwall, was settled in what was still Indian country in 1763 by families seeking to make fortunes in the New World by cutting the great tall pines of the region to provide masts for the Royal Navy. Almost immediately, however, the town, despite its remote location and rugged landscape, began to distinguish itself among its neighbors because of the achievements of the Chase family, who dominated the community in its early years and finally produced, after many other distinguished members, Salmon

Portland Chase, a Republican contender for the presidency in 1860, who became Lincoln's secretary of the Treasury and then chief justice of the U.S. Supreme Court from 1864 to 1873.

The general decline of upper New England after the Civil War and the passage of the Homestead Act, which encouraged farmers to move West, threatened Cornish, which dropped from a population of 1,520 in 1860 to 934 in 1890, slightly less than its population of 982 a century before.[4] Cornish, however, was spared the dour fate that turned much of upper New England into a backdrop for forbidding literary works like Edith Wharton's *Ethan Frome* and Robert Frost's "Home Burial" by two almost storybook events that brought it international distinction.

On the east side of town, New York investment banker Austin Corbin, who never lived in Cornish but in the Sullivan County seat of Newport, across the Blue Mountains, began in 1886 acquiring abandoned farms for what has become the largest private game park in the United States, boasting exotic quarry like wild boar and elk for tycoon sportsmen, while also providing protection for native bison threatened with extinction. The Blue Mountain Forest Association is still the largest landholder in the town.

Meanwhile, crosstown along the Connecticut River, a quite different development was involving people with similar backgrounds to the wealthy sportsmen. Charles Colesworth Beaman, Jr., "a highly successful leader of the New York bar like his father-in-law [William Maxwell Evarts],"[5] acquired most of the land from the covered bridge to the northern town line with Plainfield and seeking the company of artists and writers, gave, rented, or sold the farm homes to friends from the city, turning the "Cornish Colony" into a "Little New York."

The most distinguished of the group to be attracted to the community was the sculptor Augustus Saint-Gaudens, whose summer home is now the national historic site. Many others like the American novelist Winston Churchill, who went on to pursue a career in New Hampshire politics, and the dramatic poet Percy MacKaye, joined him. President Theodore Roosevelt hunted in Corbin's Park in 1902, and President Woodrow Wilson rented "Harlakenden," Churchill's house, as the summer White House for the three years of 1913-15 before the United States became involved in World War I.

Best known of the group in later years was Maxfield Parrish, who though he built his home "The Oaks" just across the town line in

Plainfield, was for many years one of the principal moving spirits of the "Cornish Colony," which flourished through the 1920s.

Local families who had benefited from the presence of the summer colony hoped that the arrival of Salinger after World War II might revive the town's past glories, but the writer shunned a social role, and few followed him, though a number of young couples also attracted by life away from the crowded cities have been restoring old farmhouses and building new homes to experiment with solar heating systems. Don Powers, a young Boston stockbroker, also bought the old general store in Cornish Flat, the principal settlement in the town, in order to raise his family in the country and develop a mail-order business.

Prospects brightened principally when retired opera singer Roberta Wells acquired Maxfield Parrish's "The Oaks" and converted the handsome drawing room with a fireplace that could hold a whole tree trunk into Wells Woods, the kind of fashionable restaurant-inn that might attract visitors to the town. The fireplace, however, proved the undoing of the scheme when, one crisp evening after a Dartmouth football game, some coals fell through the loosened plaster in the back wall of the fireplace and started a blaze that destroyed the regional treasure house. It has been restored to its former exterior appearance by a Mexican papal countess, who has also expanded a museum of Parrish's work, but the restaurant has not resumed operation. Augustus Saint-Gaudens's work is also on display in his former studio, where other regional art exhibits are also presented during the summer. A few of the creative workers at Dartmouth College have also moved to Cornish, though most of them cluster around Thetford, Vermont, some distance to the north. Although Salinger is a presence felt but not seen, the town remains an unusually distinguished cultural center for such a small, remote community.

Its achievement is all the more remarkable for its taking a hardy soul to survive the Cornish year, especially where Salinger lives high in the hills. The summer is glorious, with a profusion of flowers that approaches Great Britain's, and there are usually only a very few hot, humid days in July. But the frost comes early, usually with the start of autumn in September, withering the still splendid stands of wild aster. October is usually the most pleasant month in the region, but there follows a long, hard winter of four months when the ground is frozen too hard even to bury the dead. Spring comes late: the resplendent lilacs do not perfume the air and delight winter-tired eyes until May.

Though the region has become much more accessible since Salinger first moved there by virtue of the construction of two of the most breathtakingly beautiful stretches of interstate highway in the country, which cross just outside White River Junction, Vermont, many families have been discouraged and broken up by the lonely isolation of the gray winter with short days and nights when the temperature may often drop to twenty-five below zero.

A consolation for someone like Salinger seeking peace and privacy is that his neighbors are, in the tradition of rural New England, very private people, slow to assimilate newcomers into their society and rigidly protective of the right to live in seclusion. Cornish is a community devoted to traditions; its local historian reports that when polled, most of the residents said they liked Cornish the way it was and did not want it changed.[6] As for Salinger, Wade comments only that he maintains an earlier resident's "tradition of isolation." The families that have lived in these hills for generations respect this tradition.

From downriver come the persistent inquiries about what Salinger is doing, is he still writing? On the rare occasions that he has chosen to say anything, he has insisted that he is, but he has denounced publication as "a terrible invasion" of his privacy. As the unpleasant termination of the 1980 interview with Betty Eppes shows, Salinger does not like to be touched physically. This episode has many implications that help to explain antisocial persons. *Touching* has in English a number of interrelated meanings. People who are uncomfortable about being touched physically, whether by someone making sexual advances or offering or seeking therapeutic assistance, usually do not like to be *touched* emotionally, either, as by a sad story—real or fictional—whether it is intended to convey a moral or exploit another's feelings for personal gain. Both physical and emotional touching can be so distressing for hypersensitive persons that they are upset to an extent more hardened people find incomprehensible. (The concluding scene of John Steinbeck's *Of Mice and Men* dramatizes this contrast especially effectively.)

Bruce Bawer quotes Ian Hamilton as documenting that Salinger was frequently condescending to others, but what gladhanders may interpret as condescension may more accurately be diagnosed as an extreme inability to relate spontaneously to other people.[7] Throughout this study, we have observed a number of examples of both Salinger's and his characters' inability to cope with situations they do not completely control. This tendency needs to be given careful consideration when raising questions about Salinger's isolated way of life. If he wants to be left alone, he should be, so long as he is also willing to leave others alone.

My guess is that he will not publish again, because he has gotten too far out of touch with the general reader. I think that he is most like the little boy in Holden Caulfield's favorite of the stories written by his brother D. B. before D. B. "prostituted" himself in Hollywood. In the story the boy will not let anyone else look at his "secret gold-fish," because he bought it with his own money. Salinger has bought his privacy with his own money; now he is entitled to enjoy it. His long silence has not affected his reputation, although the passage of time has made it clearer that it is likely to rest principally on *The Catcher in the Rye.*

I do not agree with James Miller, Jr., (who may no longer think what he did in 1965) that Salinger occupies "perhaps the pre-eminent position" in post–World War II American fiction. I think that honor should go, with some ironic justice, to Ralph Ellison for *Invisible Man,* which I think in a long perspective may come to be seen as the *Moby-Dick* of the American twentieth century. Ellison provides an interesting comparison with Salinger, because his reputation has also not suffered from not following up on his first novel, which was published soon after *The Catcher in the Rye.* Although Ellison has since led a much more public life than Salinger, I think that there is a somewhat similar reason for his long silence. At the end of *Invisible Man,* the unnamed narrator says that he may some day emerge from his underground cave of light if he feels he has a responsible role to play in society. I think that Ellison has not returned to the story, because that time has not yet come, just as Salinger's novel still remains popular because the situation it depicts has only worsened. Our society remains still the one that Holden grudgingly accepted and that Ellison's invisible man fled for his life. The only difference is that right at the moment of this writing, we are calling the pursuers "yuppies."

Salinger did try to evoke an alternative life-style in the Glass family stories; but these tales that are more idealistic than *Catcher* seem today to have less relevance to those who lead what Thoreau called "lives of quiet desperation," because as some astute critics like John Updike long ago recognized they are nostalgic souvenirs of a time when people thought they might find a panacea. Salinger avoided the fashionable furor over Miltown, lobotomies, and LSD; but even the path that his later characters follow of Christian prayer or the way of Tao have lost their appeal because of the overreaching of Dr. Moon and other emissaries from the Orient as well as our own television evangelists. Even Saint Seymour ends up telling people what to do instead of inspiring them to work out their own salvations. Salinger has presumably been testing other roads since then, but it would be indeed a terrible invasion of his privacy to insist on following him along them without being invited. The most admirable characters he created remain Lady Esmé and the pseudonymous "De Daumier-Smith." We really do not need to know why he left them behind, because he left them behind for us.

Notes and References

Preface

1. The other novel is James T. Farrell's *Studs Lonigan* trilogy; the other five books are Walter Lippmann's *Drift and Mastery,* the report by Alfred P. Sloan (1920) that revolutionized American industrial management, Dale Carnegie's *How to Win Friends and Influence People,* Dr. Benjamin Spock's *Baby and Child Care,* and the first volume of the Kinsey report, *Sexual Behavior in the Human Male.* All of these essays have been landmarks in revealing or redirecting the American life-style.

Chapter One

1. Quoted in Eberhard Alsen, *Salinger's Glass Stories as a Composite Novel* (Troy, N.Y.: Whitston, 1983), 187. Subsequent page references follow in the text.

2. [Jack Skow], "Sonny: An Introduction," *Time,* 15 September 1961, 88.

3. Bruce Bawer, "Salinger's Arrested Development," *New Criterion* 5 (September 1986):35.

4. Frederick Pillsbury, "Mysterious J. D. Salinger: The Untold Chapter of the Famous Writer's Years as a Valley Forge Cadet," Philadelphia *Sunday Bulletin Magazine,* 29 October 1961, 23–24.

5. Shirley Blaney, "Twin State Telescope," Claremont [New Hampshire] *Daily Eagle,* 13 November 1953, 1; Betty Eppes, "What I Did Last Summer," *Paris Review* 80, 24 July 1981, 237.

6. Jack R. Sublette, *J. D. Salinger: An Annotated Bibliography: 1938–81* (New York: Garland, 1984), 25.

7. Carlos Baker, *Ernest Hemingway: A Life Story* (New York: Scribner's, 1969), 646.

8. "Epilogue: A Salute to Whit Burnett, 1899–1972," in Hallie and Whit Burnett, *Fiction Writer's Handbook* (New York: Harper and Row, 1975), 187–88.

9. Sublette, *Salinger,* 59.

10. Ibid., 25, 59.

11. Skow, "Sonny," 88; Bawer, "Salinger's Development," 35.

12. Bawer, 35.

13. Bawer, "Salinger's Development," 35; Sublette, *Salinger,* 25.

14. All details from Pillsbury, "Mysterious Salinger," 23–24.

15. William Maxwell, "J. D. Salinger," *Book-of-the-Month Club News,*

Midsummer 1951, 6; reprinted in *The Book of the Month: Sixty Years of Books in American Life*, ed. Al Silverman (Boston: Little, Brown, 1986), 125–30.

16. Ibid.

17. Eppes, "What I Did," 237.

18. William Poster, "Tomorrow's Child," *Commentary* 13 (January 1952):90–92. See Malcolm M. Marsden, *If You Really Want to Know: A "Catcher" Casebook* (Chicago: Scott Foresman, 1963) for a representative collection of early reviews by Virigilia Peterson, Paul Engle, Harvey Breit, Harrison Smith, and others.

19. Eloise Perry Hazard, "Eight Fictional Finds," *Saturday Review*, 16 February 1952, 17.

20. Robert Gutwilling, "Everybody's Caught 'The Catcher in the Rye,'" *New York Times Book Review*, 15 January 1961, 38.

21. Joseph Blotner, *Faulkner: A Biography*, 2 vols. (New York: Random House, 1974), 2:1604.

22. Bawer, "Salinger's Development," 39.

23. Skow, "Sonny," 89.

24. Alsen, *Salinger's Glass Stories*, 143–58, provides the fullest account of these doctrines, as explained by Salinger's teachers.

25. John Updike, "Anxious Days for the Glass Family," *New York Times Book Review*, 17 September 1961; reprinted in *Salinger: A Critical and Personal Portrait*, ed. Henry Anatole Grunwald (New York: Harper and Brothers, 1962), 53–56.

26. See Sandra Gray, "Newsmakers," *Newsweek*, 12 October 1981, 113, for details about Matt's theatrical training and career.

27. Hugh Mason Wade, *A Brief History of Cornish, 1763–1974* (Hanover, N.H.: University Press of New England, 1976), 93–94.

28. *Town of Cornish 1978 Real Estate Assessment.* One of a series of annual pamphlets signed by the Selectmen of Cornish. The curious can obtain updates from the Selectmen's Office. The public library in Cornish Flat also archives small-scale maps of the town, showing the locations of all buildings and property holdings.

29. Sublette, *Salinger*, 59.

30. Eppes, "What I Did," 238.

31. Ibid.

32. Lacey Fosburgh, "J. D. Salinger Speaks about His Silence," *New York Times*, 3 November 1974, 1, 69.

33. [London] *Sunday Times*, 12 October 1986, 4e; *Times Literary Supplement*, 14 November 1986, 1267d.

34. Patricia Miller, "Between the Lines," [London] *Sunday Times*, 15 November 1987, 51. The book was published as *In Search of J.D. Salinger* (New York: Random House) in May 1988; excerpts in *Vanity Fair*, May 1988, 158–172.

35. [London] *Sunday Times*, 18 January 1987, 11a; an especially amus-

ing international view of the geriatric struggle for control of the magazine appeared in [London] *Literary Review,* March 1987, 47.

36. Barbara Graustark, "Newsmakers," *Newsweek,* 17 July 1978, 57. In June 1982, Salinger also made a much publicized trip to Jacksonville, Florida, to see Elaine Joyce in *6 Rms Riv Vu* at the Alhambra Dinner Theater, though no further dalliance was reported (*International Herald Tribune,* 15 June 1982; the report incorrectly places his home in Vermont).

Chapter Two

1. Bawer, "Salinger's Development," 39, note.

2. Sublette, *Salinger,* 21, reports that "Two Lonely Men" in the *Story* archives at Columbia University is about an adulterous wife at a southern U.S. Army base during World War II. Other stories in the archive are "The Children's Echelon," from the diary of eighteen-year-old Bernice Herndon; "The Magic Foxhole," a story of D day; and "The Ocean Full of Bowling Balls," Vincent Caulfield's story about his brother Kenneth's death.

3. "The Young Folks," *Story,* March-April 1940, 30.

4. The other member of this much-publicized pair was Brenda Duff Frazier.

5. "The Long Debut of Lois Taggett," *Story,* September-October 1942, 34.

6. "Once a Week Won't Kill You," *Story,* November-December 1944, 26.

7. Sublette, *Salinger,* 30. Salinger also wrote Whit Burnett in 1943 about selling the movies a story called "Rex Passad on the Planet Mars" that has never been located and is not elsewhere mentioned.

8. "The Varioni Brothers," *Saturday Evening Post,* 17 July 1943, 77.

9. "Both Parties Concerned," *Saturday Evening Post,* 20 February 1944, 14.

10. Sublette, *Salinger,* 30.

11. "A Young Girl in 1941 with no Waist at All," *Mademoiselle,* May 1947, 222. (Actually the only film the trio made about West Point was *Flirtation Walk* but they appeared in a number of Warner Brothers' 1930s musicals.)

12. Ibid., 302.

13. "Blue Melody," *Cosmopolitan,* September 1948, 112.

14. Frederick L. Gwynn and Joseph L. Blotner, *Faulkner at the University* (Charlottesville: University of Virginia Press, 1959), 244. Faulkner rated *The Catcher in the Rye* as the best novel he had read of the present generation, perhaps because it "expresses so completely" what he had tried to say.

15. "A Girl I Knew," *Good Housekeeping,* February 1948, 190.

16. Charles J. Rolo, "The New Bohemia," *Flair,* February 1950, 27.

Rolo, staff literary critic, is introduced as a lecturer at Columbia University (15). New Bohemians besides Capote and Williams included Gore Vidal, Jane and Paul Bowles, Speed Lamkin, and Theodora Keogh (of the Roosevelt clan). Salinger is nowhere mentioned, and *Flair* did not last long enough to greet the publication of *The Catcher in the Rye*.

17. "The Inverted Forest," *Cosmopolitan,* Diamond Jubilee Issue, March 1961, 115. Page references follow in the text.

18. Frederick L. Gwynn and Joseph L. Blotner, *The Fiction of J. D. Salinger* (Pittsburgh, Pa.: University of Pittsburgh Press, 1958), 14.

19. Kenneth Hamilton, *J. D. Salinger: A Critical Essay* (Grand Rapids, Mich.: Eerdmans, 1967), 18.

20. Paul Levine, "J. D. Salinger: The Development of the Misfit Hero," *Twentieth Century Literature* 4 (October 1958):93–94.

21. Bawer, "Salinger's Development," 35. Immediately subsequent page references follow in text.

22. Lois Gordon and Alan Gordon, *American Chronicle: Six Decades in American Life 1920–1980* (New York: Atheneum, 1987), 196. This remarkable compendium, spanning the Salinger years, is an indispensable source of information for understanding the historical context of Salinger's writings, which were heavily influenced by popular culture. Joe Kelly's "Quiz Kids," with panelists under sixteen, is listed as premiering in 1940, part of a new genre that had been launched in 1936 with Craig Earl's "Professor Quiz" program. By that year Seymour Glass was receiving his Ph.D. from Columbia University.

Chapter Three

1. Herschel Brickell, "Backstage with Esquire," *Esquire,* October 1945, 34.

2. Bawer, "Salinger's Development," 41.

3. Blaney, "Twin State Telescope," 1.

4. Sublett, *Salinger,* 30.

5. Maxwell, "Salinger," 6.

6. "Last Day of the Last Furlough," *Saturday Evening Post,* 15 July 1944, 61.

7. *The Catcher in the Rye* (Boston: Little, Brown, 1951), 13. Page references to this first edition follow in the text.

8. In "Salinger in the Waste Land," *Modern Fiction Studies* 12 (Autumn 1966):367–79, John M. Howell draws fascinating parallels between both the theme and structure of Eliot's *Waste Land* and *The Catcher in the Rye*. Just how conscious Salinger may have been of a sequence of remarkable parallels is one of those matters, like some discussed in Chapter Four of this book, that even the author might not be able to speak of with certainty. "The Inverted Forest" makes it clear that Salinger knew Eliot's poem and used it as a source of

allusions. Since both works are classic examples of what are discussed in this text as rituals of *deinitiation*, striking similarities may be expected from writers approaching the material from similar cultural backgrounds. Howell's essay, however, remains of unique significance in placing Salinger's colloquial novel unmistakably in the aristocratic tradition of "Waste Land" literature.

9. "I'm Crazy," *Collier's*, 22 December 1945, 51.

10. "Slight Rebellion Off Madison," *New Yorker*, 21 December 1946, 77. The conversation in *Catcher* (169) is wordier, but contains the same essential terms.

11. Eppes, "What I Did," 238. Salinger completely lost his cool when a bookstore owner rushed out and tried to shake his hand, and in Eppes's words, "chewed my ass out."

12. John W. Aldridge, *In Search of Heresy* (New York: McGraw-Hill, 1956), 130–31.

13. Mark David Chapman murdered former Beatle John Lennon in December 1980 on a Manhattan street near the famous Dakota apartment house on Central Park West, where Lennon and his family had taken up residence in New York. Chapman was a Lennon fan and a Salinger fan. At his trial, he claimed that Lennon was about to be corrupted by "commercialism" and that Chapman was protecting Lennon's innocence. At his sentencing, Chapman read Holden's "catcher in the rye" speech in justification of his action. Daniel M. Stashower argues in "On First Looking into Chapman's Holden: Speculations on a Murder," *American Scholar* 52 (1983):373–77, that Chapman took Holden's speech as dogma, not realizing that Salinger's character had matured enough to realize the authoritarian fallacy of his fantasy (see page 17).

14. I most recently encountered "fuck you" scratched into the stone sill of the "public conveniences" at St. David's, Wales, where it cannot be missed by the small children from all over the world visiting the great cathedral.

15. Quotations are in Freese's original English from *English and American Studies in German: Summaries of Theses*, Supplement to *Anglia*, ed. Werner Habicht (Tübingen, Germany: Max Niemeyer Verlag, 1972), item 88, pp. 175–78.

16. Malcolm Cowley, *The Faulkner-Cowley File* (New York: Viking Press, 1966), 16.

17. Silverman, ed., *Book of the Month*, 127.

18. See Chapter One, no. 18.

19. R. G. G. Price, "Booking Office," *Punch*, 18 August 1951.

20. William Dean Howells, *The Rise of Silas Lapham*, in *A Selected Edition of William Dean Howells*, (Bloomington: Indiana University Press, 1971), 12:361.

21. Silverman, ed. *Book of the Month*, 128.

22. United States Information Service, "American Top Twelve," (ca. 1963), 46–48. My copy is from a clipping file that does not name the periodical, though the date is, from adjacent reviews, almost surely July 1963.

130   J. D. SALINGER

23. Gerald Rosen, "A Retrospective Look at *The Catcher in the Rye*," *American Quarterly* 29 (Winter 1977):561. Page references follow in text.

24. Theodore Roszak's *Making of a Counter Culture: Reflections on the Technocratic Society and Its Youthful Opposition* (Garden City, N.Y.: Doubleday, 1969) makes no mention of Salinger or his writings even in a chapter on "Journey to the East . . . and Points Beyond," devoted principally to Allen Ginsberg and Alan Watts.

25. James Purdy, *Malcolm* (New York: Farrar, Straus & Cudahy, 1959), 8. Purdy's distaste for *The Catcher in the Rye* is indicated by some parodic remarks in *Cabot Wright Begins* (1964).

26. Carol and Richard Ohmann, "Reviewers, Critics, and *The Catcher in the Rye*," *Critical Inquiry* 3 (Autumn 1976):15. Page references follow in the text. James E. Miller, Jr.'s reply appeared in *Critical Inquiry* 3 (Spring 1977):599–603, and the Ohmanns' rebuttal in *Critical Inquiry* 3 (Summer 1977):773–77.

27. Faulkner sees the alternatives as preferring death (like Seymour Glass), refusing to participate (as Salinger has), or trying to clean up the mess. Faulkner goes on to say that Isaac McCaslin in "The Bear" chose the second course, but that we need people who will choose the third ("A Word to Young Writers" in Gwynn and Blotner, *Faulkner at the University*, 243–47).

28. Vera Panova, "On J. D. Salinger's Novel," trans. Carl Proffer, *Soviet Criticism of American Literature in the Sixties: An Anthology*, ed. Carl R. Proffer (Ann Arbor, Mich.: ARDIS, 1972), 4–10.

29. David Riesman, Nathan Glazer, and Reuel Denney, *The Lonely Crowd: A Study in the Changing American Character* (Garden City, N.Y.: Doubleday Anchor, 1953). Page references follow in the text.

30. A community of more than a hundred hippies was, for example, ordered in August 1987 to leave a Teepee Village near Llandello in southwest Wales that it had been occupying for ten years (*South Wales Evening Post*, 12 August 1987, 1; [London] *Times*, 13 August 1987, 5). Hippie caravans still regularly convene on Midsummer's Eve near Stonehenge.

31. Christopher Lasch, *The Culture of Narcissism: American Life in an Age of Diminishing Expectations* (New York: Warner Books, 1979), 21. Page references follow in the text.

Chapter Four

1. For undisclosed reasons, the British edition of *Nine Stories* was retitled *"For Esmé—With Love and Squalor" and Other Stories* and a change was made in the order of the stories by placing "Just before the War with the Eskimos" fifth in the collection instead of third as in the American edition and moving "The Laughing Man" and "Down at the Dinghy" to the third and fourth positions respectively. The title change is easy to understand because "For Esmé" was Salinger's first story to be published in a British magazine (*World*

Review, August 1950), and it presented an affectionate view of a titled British teenager, so that it could be expected to have great drawing power. I can offer no theories about the slight change in the order of the stories, although I would prefer that those who wish to test my theories about the story cycle would read them in the original order of the American edition. (I have not checked the order of the stories in various translations of the collection.)

2. Forrest L. Ingram, *Representative Short-Story Cycles of the Twentieth Century* (The Hague: Mouton, 1971), 15.

3. *"Raise High the Roof Beam, Carpenters" and "Seymour: An Introduction"* (Boston: Little, Brown, 1963), 123. Page references follow in the text.

4. *Nine Stories* (Boston: Little, Brown, 1953), 12. Page references follow in the text.

5. One of the most detailed accounts of "The Influence of Hindu-Buddhist Psychology and Philosophy on J. D. Salinger's Fiction" is Hamayun Ali Mirza's unpublished Ph.D. dissertation of that title (State University of New York at Binghamton, 1976), which reaches the conclusion that "ultimately, in the Glass saga, the function of the East is to awaken the West to its own inner reservoir of spirituality and perennial wisdom" (*Dissertation Abstracts International* 37A (August 1976), no. 2, p. 971). I have not summarized Mirza's complicated exegesis, because his dissertation is available on microfilm. I am drawing here, however, on a paper that Mirza, a former student, subsequently sent me for comment, in which he developed his thesis of Seymour as a false guru, whose spiritual development is arrested by his sensuality (maya). Unfortunately, this paper has not been published, nor have I been able to consult further with Dr. Mirza. His theories underlie, however, my own conception of the *Nine Stories* as a story cycle, first outlined in the entry for Salinger, "American Novelists since World War II," *Dictionary of Literary Biography*, vol. 2 (Detroit: Gale Research, 1978).

6. Alsen, *Salinger's Glass Stories*, 147.

7. Richard Allan Davison, "Salinger Criticism and 'The Laughing Man': A Case of Arrested Development," *Studies in Short Fiction* 18 (Winter 1981):1–15. Davison questions my emphasis on the narrator's "rite of passage," but the narrator is the only character that we can begin to understand, for we have access only to his thoughts, and he comments that he has no idea what happened between the Chief and Mary.

8. John Edward Hardy, *Commentaries on Five Modern American Short Stories* (Frankfurt am Main: Athenaum, 1962), 7–10.

9. Ihab Hassan, *Radical Innocence: Studies in the Contemporary American Novel* (Princeton, N.J.: Princeton University Press, 1961), 263.

10. See Allen Ginsberg, "The Art of Poetry VIII," *Paris Review* 37 (Spring 1966):42–43, for Ginsberg's account of a transformational experience in the more dignified setting of a bookstore; for a detailed analysis of Ginsberg's experience, see Thomas F. Merrill, *Allen Ginsberg*, rev. ed. (Boston: Twayne, 1988).

11. Gwynn and Blotner, *Fiction of Salinger,* 33–42.

12. Stephen Crane, *The Red Badge of Courage.* The University of Virginia Edition of the Works of Stephen Crane 10 vols. (Charlottesville: University of Virginia Press, 1969), 2:135.

13. See Warren French, "Stephen Crane: Moment of Myth," *Prairie Schooner* 55 (Spring/Summer 1951):155–67, for an account of the relationship of "The Veteran" to *The Red Badge of Courage.*

14. "Blue Melody," *Cosmopolitan,* September 1948, 112. See discussion of this story in Chapter Two.

15. Another fascinating possible basis for a cyclical pattern in the nine stories remains to be explored. In a paper unpublished at the time of this writing, James Finn Cotter suggests a parallel between the poems in Rilke's *Das Buch der Bilder* ("The Book of Images," bk. 2, pt. 2) and the stories, examining "The Song of the Suicide" especially as a source for "A Perfect Day for Bananafish."

16. Updike, "Anxious Days," 56.

Chapter Five

1. Updike, "Anxious Days," 53.

2. *Franny and Zooey* (Boston: Little, Brown, 1961), 32. Page references follow in the text.

3. Alsen, *Salinger's Glass Stories,* 21, follows Updike in summing up the evidence that "Franny" was written before Salinger's plan for the Glass family series had taken shape.

4. Skow, "Sonny," 89.

5. Alsen, *Salinger's Glass Stories,* xi–xii.

6. See Warren French, *Jack Kerouac* (Boston: Twayne, 1986), xi, 43 for comments on similarities between Kerouac's and Salinger's lives and fiction.

7. Updike, "Anxious Days," 56.

8. Kerry McSweeney, "Salinger Revisited," *Critical Quarterly* 20, no. 1 (Spring 1978):61–68.

9. Alsen, *Salinger's Glass Stories,* 227.

10. Updike, "Anxious Days," 56.

11. Warren French, *J. D. Salinger* (New York: Twayne, 1963) 147–48. After twenty-five years, I doubt that a final comparison made then with the works of Emile Coué means much any more.

Chapter Six

1. Updike, "Anxious Days," 55. Page references follow in the text.

2. Alsen, *Salinger's Glass Stories,* 33. Page references follow in the text.

3. See McSweeney "Salinger Revisited," for a further analysis of Fitzgerald's influence.

4. Mary McCarthy, "J. D. Salinger's Closed Circuit," *Harper's Magazine,* October 1962, 47.

5. Ibid.

6. Maxwell, "Salinger," 6.

7. I am disinclined to accept Truman Capote's gossipy report to Lawrence Grobel (*Conversations with Capote* [New York: New American Library, 1985], 147–48) that Salinger had written at least five or six "very strange" short novels, "all about Zen Buddhism" that the *New Yorker* had refused to publish. As Alsen, *Salinger's Glass Stories,* 167–68, points out, despite the epigraph to *Nine Stories,* Zen plays only a small role in Salinger's work, which has been principally rooted in Advaita Vedanta. The author of *Breakfast at Tiffany's* and his coterie were probably little bothered about distinguishing between exotic mystiques; but his report should be cited as likely to be one of the most influential, if worthless, about Salinger's activities since 1965.

Chapter Seven

1. Wade, *Brief History,* 93.

2. Ibid.

3. *Kansas City Star,* (AP report), 15 November 1967, 2. She was also awarded eight thousand dollars a year in support. In the divorce suit, she charged "treatment 'to injure health and endanger reason.'"

4. Wade, *Brief History,* 40.

5. Ibid., 44.

6. Ibid., 1.

7. Bawer, "Salinger's Development," 38.

Selected Bibliography

PRIMARY SOURCES

1. *Books*

The Catcher in the Rye. Boston: Little, Brown & Co., 1951. Reprints. New York: Grosset and Dunlap, 1952; New York: New American Library (paperback), 1953; New York: Modern Library, 1958; New York: Bantam Books (paperback), 1964.

Franny and Zooey. Boston: Little, Brown & Co., 1961. Reprint. New York: Bantam Books (paperback), 1964.

Nine Stories. Boston: Little, Brown & Co., 1953. Reprints. New York: New American Library (paperback), 1954; New York: Modern Library, 1959; New York: Bantam Books (paperback), 1964. British edition. *For Esmé— With Love and Squalor and Other Stories.* London: Hamish Hamilton, 1955.

Raise High the Roof Beam, Carpenters and Seymour: An Introduction. Boston: Little, Brown & Co., 1963. Reprint. New York: Bantam Books (paperback), 1965.

Note: An unauthorized paperbound *Complete Uncollected Short Stories of J. D. Salinger* appeared in two volumes, containing the twenty-two stories not included in the three authorized collections. It was apparently published by unidentified parties in Berkeley, California, as reported in the *New York Times,* 3 November 1974, 1. It has been suppressed by the copyright holders.

2. *Short Stories*

"Blue Melody." *Cosmopolitan,* September 1948, 50–51, 112–19.

"Both Parties Concerned." *Saturday Evening Post,* 20 February 1944, 14, 47–48.

"A Boy in France." *Saturday Evening Post,* 31 March 1945, 21, 92; Reprint in *Post Stories, 1942–1945,* edited by Ben Hibbs (New York: Random House, 1946), 314–20.

"De Daumier-Smith's Blue Period." [London] *World Review,* n. s., no. 39 (May 1952):33–48. Reprint in *Nine Stories,* 130–65.

"Down at the Dinghy." *Harper's,* April 1949, 87–91. Reprint in *Nine Stories,* 74–86.

"Elaine." *Story,* March-April 1945, 38–47.

"For Esmé—With Love and Squalor." *New Yorker,* 8 April 1950, 28–36. Reprint in [London] *World Review,* n. s., no. 18 (August 1950):44–59; *Prize*

Stories of 1950: The O. Henry Awards, edited by Herschel Brickell (Garden City, N.Y.: Doubleday, 1950), 244–64; *Fifty Great Short Stories,* edited by Milton Crane (New York: Bantam Books, 1952); *Nine Stories,* 87–114; and in several college textbooks.

"Franny." *New Yorker,* 29 January, 1955, 24–43. Reprint in *Franny and Zooey,* 3–43.

"A Girl I Knew." *Good Housekeeping,* February 1948, 37, 186–96. Reprint in *Best American Short Stories of 1949,* edited by Martha J. Foley (Boston: Houghton Mifflin, 1949), 248–60.

"Go See Eddie." *University of Kansas City Review* 7 (December 1940):121–24.

"The Hang of It." *Collier's,* 12 July 1941, 22.

"Hapworth 16, 1924," *New Yorker,* 19 June 1965, 32–113.

"The Heart of a Broken Story." *Esquire,* September 1941, 32, 131–33.

"I'm Crazy." *Collier's,* 22 December 1945, 36, 48, 51. (Some material from this story included in *The Catcher in the Rye.*)

"The Inverted Forest." *Cosmopolitan,* December 1947, 73–109. Reprint in *Cosmopolitan,* Diamond Jubilee Issue, March 1961, 111–32.

"Just before the War with the Eskimos." *New Yorker,* 5 June 1948, 37–46. Reprint in *Prize Stories of 1949,* edited by Herschel Brickell (Garden City, N.Y.: Doubleday, 1949), 249–61; *Nine Stories,* 39–55; *Manhattan: Stories from the Heart of a Great City,* edited by Seymour Krim (New York: Bantam Books, 1954), 22–35.

"Last Day of the Last Furlough." *Saturday Evening Post,* 15 July 1944, 26–27, 61–64.

"The Laughing Man." *New Yorker,* 19 March 1949, 27–32. Reprinted in *Nine Stories,* 56–73.

"The Long Debut of Lois Taggett." *Story,* September-October 1942, 28–34. Reprint in *Story: The Fiction of the Forties,* edited by Whit and Hallie S. Burnett (New York: Dutton, 1949), 153–62.

"Once a Week Won't Kill You." *Story,* November-December 1944, 23–27.

"A Perfect Day for Bananafish." *New Yorker,* 31 January 1948, 21–25. Reprint in *55 Short Stories from the New Yorker* (New York: Simon and Schuster, 1949), 144–45; *Nine Stories,* 3–18.

"Personal Notes of an Infantryman." *Collier's,* 12 December 1942, 96.

"Pretty Mouth and Green My Eyes." *New Yorker,* 14 July 1951, 20–24. Reprint in *Anthology of Famous American Short Stories,* edited by J. A. Burrell and Bennett Cerf (New York: Modern Library, 1953), 1297–1306; *Nine Stories,* 115–29.

"Raise High the Roof Beam, Carpenters." *New Yorker,* 10 November 1955, 51–116. Reprint in *Short Stories from the New Yorker, 1950–1960* (New York: Simon and Schuster, 1960), 49–65; as a book with "Seymour: An Introduction," 3–107.

"Seymour: An Introduction." *New Yorker,* 6 June 1959, 42–111. Reprint in book with "Raise High the Roof Beam, Carpenters," 111–248.

"Slight Rebellion Off Madison." *New Yorker,* 21 December 1946, 76–79. (Some material from this story included in *The Catcher in the Rye.*)

"Soft-Boiled Sergeant." *Saturday Evening Post,* 15 April 1944, 82–85.

"The Stranger." *Collier's,* 1 December 1945, 18, 77.

"Teddy." *New Yorker,* 31 January 1953, 26–38. Reprint in *Nine Stories,* 166–98.

"This Sandwich Has No Mayonnaise." *Esquire,* October 1945, 54–56, 147–49. Reprint in *The Armchair Esquire,* edited by Arnold Gingrich and L. Rust Hills (New York: Putnam's, 1958), 187–97.

"Uncle Wiggily in Connecticut." *New Yorker,* 20 March 1948, 30–36. Reprint in *Short Story Masterpieces,* edited by Robert Penn Warren and Albert Erskine (New York: Dell, 1954), 408–23. *Nine Stories,* 19–38.

"The Varioni Brothers." *Saturday Evening Post,* 17 July 1943, 12–13, 76–77.

"The Young Folks." *Story,* March-April 1940, 26–30.

"A Young Girl in 1941 with No Waist at All." *Mademoiselle,* May 1947, 222–23, 292–302.

"Zooey." *New Yorker,* 4 May 1957, 32–139. Reprint in *Franny and Zooey,* 47–201.

3. *Miscellaneous Prose*

"Epilogue: A Salute to Whit Burnett, 1899–1972." In Hallie and Whit Burnett, *Fiction Writer's Handbook* (New York: Harper and Row, 1975), 187–88. (A tribute to the editor of *Story* and Salinger's teacher in a short-story writing class at Columbia University in 1939, originally intended for *Story Jubilee: 33 Years of "Story"* [1965].)

"Man-Forsaken Man." *New York Post Magazine,* 9 December 1955, 49. (A copy of a letter to Governor Nelson Rockefeller of New York, lamenting the condition of men sentenced to state prisons for life.)

4. *Unpublished stories*

Jack Sublette describes five unpublished stories in the *Story* magazine archives at Columbia University—"The Children's Echelon," "The Last and Best of the Peter Pans," "The Magic Foxhole," "The Ocean Full of Bowling Balls," and "Two Lonely Men," only the last of these signed Jerry Salinger. (*An Annotated Bibliography: 1938–1981* [New York: Garland, 1984], 21.) See Chapter Two, n. 2.

SECONDARY SOURCES

1. *Bibliography*

Beebe, Maurice, and Jennifer Sperry. "Criticism of J. D. Salinger: A Selected Checklist." *Modern Fiction Studies,* 12, no. 3 (Autumn 1966):377–

90. In need of updating, this compilation for a special Salinger issue of the quarterly is still indispensable for its story-by-story breakdown of the relevant criticism in books and articles in English.

Sublette, Jack R. *J. D. Salinger: An Annotated Bibliography: 1938–1981* (New York: Garland, 1984). A compilation of materials through 1982 that supplants all previous listings and should require only updating supplements in the future. Sublette lists English editions and translations of Salinger's work (*The Catcher in the Rye* has been translated into twenty-nine languages and exists in two versions in eight of these), critical books and articles in English and other languages, and as well as book reviews, and describes the materials relating to Salinger in the *Story* archives at Columbia University.

2. Biography

Bawer, Bruce. "Salinger's Arrested Development." *New Criterion* 5 (September 1986):34–47. An extraordinary source of information intended as a review of Ian Hamilton's biography, prepared from an advance copy of the book and circulated before the publication was delayed. It summarizes information from the book and analyzes critically Hamilton's approach, while offering the reviewer's own provocative theories.

Eppes, Betty. "What I Did Last Summer." *Paris Review*, 80 (24 July 1981):221–39. The account of a strangely staged interview in Windsor, Vermont, to which Salinger inexplicably consented in June 1980 and during which the reporter from Baton Rouge, Louisiana, took unauthorized photographs and made a secret tape recording; it contains little new information, but provides the best available glimpse of the aging Salinger's temper.

Fosburgh, Lacey. "J. D. Salinger Speaks about His Silence." *New York Times*, 3 November 1974, 1, 69. A report by the San Francisco representative of the *Times* about the only interview (by telephone) that Salinger has initiated, protesting the unauthorized publication of his short stories and describing publication as "a terrible invasion of my privacy."

Hamilton, Ian. *In Search of J. D. Salinger.* New York: Random House, 1988. Because of two rewritings necessitated by court orders to eliminate material Salinger considered privileged, this first book-length biography tells more about Hamilton's problems writing it than about its subject.

Maxwell, William. "J. D. Salinger." *Book-of-the-Month Club News*, Midsummer 1951, 5–6. An admiring account by a fellow *New Yorker* contributor with Salinger's cooperation, of his career up to the publication of *The Catcher in the Rye*.

Pillsbury, Frederick. "Mysterious J. D. Salinger: The Untold Chapter of the Famous Writer's Years as a Valley Forge Cadet." Philadelphia *Sunday Bulletin Magazine*, 29 October 1961, 23–24. The best-documented account of any period in Salinger's life drawn from the official records of the Valley Forge Military Academy in Pennsylvania, which he attended from 1934 to 1936 when he was fifteen to seventeen years of age.

[Skow, Jack]. "Sonny: An Introduction." *Time*, 15 September 1961, 84–90. The most detailed account of Salinger's life up to the peak of his celebrity with the publication of *Franny and Zooey*, assembled from the files of the newsmagazine's famous research staff. The article appears in Grunwald (see *Collections* below), credited to Skow; but one has to go back to the original publication to appreciate the period flavor created by the cover portrait, which annoyed Salinger, and the William de Kooning-like impressions of Holden Caulfield, Franny, Zooey, and Bessie Glass in the text.

3. Criticism: Books

Alsen, Eberhard. *Salinger's Glass Stories as a Composite Novel.* Troy, N.Y.: Whitston, 1983. The only monograph devoted to the Glass family stories, this book explains two ways in which they can be read as chapters of a composite novel narrating either Buddy Glass's growth as a writer or Seymour's spiritual growth. It contains also the fullest account anywhere of Salinger's interest in and use of Advaita Vedanta, composed with the help of his teachers.

Coy, Juan José. *Jerome David Salinger.* Barcelona: Fontanella, 1968. A sensitive and perceptive study of Salinger by a Spanish priest and scholar who compares Salinger to European novelists as one of the most universally significant writers about adolescence. Coy also discusses Salinger extensively in *Criteria literaria actual: Metoda y sistema* (Madrid: Editorial razon y fesa, 1966).

Freese, Peter. *Die amerikanische Kurzgeschichte nach 1945: Salinger, Malamud, Baldwin, Purdy, Barth.* Frankfurt am Main: Athenaum, 1974. Although other writers are discussed in the book, the hundred-page account of Salinger's short stories is the longest account of his artistry in the genre in any language.

————.*Die Initiationreise: Studien zum jugendlichen Helden im modernen amerikanischen Roman, mit einer exemplarischen Analyse von J. D. Salingers "The Catcher in the Rye."* Neumünster, Germany: Wachholtz, 1971. A dissertation using Salinger's novel as exemplary of the traditional narrative of the journey of initiation through many centuries and many national cultures. Together these two studies constitute the longest interpretation of the universal significance of Salinger's work published anywhere.

Gwynn, Frederick L., and Joseph L. Blotner. *The Fiction of J. D. Salinger.* Pittsburgh, Pa.: University of Pittsburgh Press, 1958. Many interpretations of individual stories in this earliest monograph about Salinger have been challenged, but it provides the best sense of the enthusiasm of his academic "discoverers" and the nature of the early response to his work.

Hamilton, Kenneth. *J. D. Salinger: A Critical Essay.* Grand Rapids, Mich.: Eerdmans, 1967. Part of a series of pamphlets on "Contemporary Writers in Christian Perspective," this sensitive reading examines the significance of Christian and other religious materials in Salinger's fiction.

Lundquist, James. *J. D. Salinger.* New York: Ungar, 1979. One of the author's several contributions to a popular series of critiques of modern literature, this book ably sums up in brief compass the principal criticism of Salinger and deals especially well with the influence of Asiatic religions on his fiction.

Miller, James E., Jr. *J. D. Salinger.* University of Minnesota Pamphlets on American Writers, no. 51. Minneapolis: University of Minnesota Press, 1965. An outstanding appreciation of Salinger's fiction by a distinguished humanist who views Salinger as the most gifted portrayer of the "alienation" that has dominated post–World War II American fiction and thus perhaps deserving of the "pre-eminent position" among its writers.

Workman, Brooke. *Writing Seminars in the Content Area: In Search of Hemingway, Salinger and Steinbeck.* Urbana, Ill.: National Council of Teachers of English, 1983. A report of an Iowa City, Iowa, high school teacher's experiments with students "Making Friends with an Author" by writing and defending a series of position papers, which ended with most of the students writing parodies, provides insights into the reactions that Salinger's fiction still generates.

4. *Criticism: Collections**

Bloom, Harold, ed. *J. D. Salinger: Modern Critical Views.* New York: Chelsea House, 1987. A selection of recent appraisals, forming part of a series, supervised by the distinguished Yale critic, to provide a guide to contemporary opinion of significant modern American writers.

Grunwald, Henry Anatole. *Salinger: A Critical and Personal Portrait.* New York: Harper and Brothers, 1962. This first gathering of original and reprinted articles contains also Jack Skow's biographical sketch and a long introduction by Grunwald, who became a senior editor of *Time.* The general tone is laudatory and conveys a sense of the enthusiasm of the Salinger cult at its height.

"J. D. Salinger Special Number." *Modern Fiction Studies,* 12, no. 3 (Autumn 1966). A collection of seven valuable articles, including Bernice and Sanford Goldstein's trail-blazing "Zen and Salinger" and the still unique Beebe and Sperry bibliography (see Section 1 above).

"Special Number: Salinger." *Wisconsin Studies in Contemporary Literature,* 4, no. 1 (Winter 1963). The first journal issue devoted to Salinger includes nine articles by such well-known Salinger critics as Ihab Hassan and Jo-

seph L. Blotner, a chapter from Warren French's not yet published book, and a bibliography by Donald Fiene, providing the earliest record of international criticism.
*Four "casebooks" for classroom use were released by different publishers in 1962 and 1963. Though long out of print, they are still valuable where they can be located. For detailed information about the contents see Sublette and the bibliography in the special issue of *Modern Fiction Studies*.

5. *Criticism: Articles and Parts of Books*
Much of the abundant criticism from the 1960s has been reprinted in collections or incorporated into later studies. Since the Sublette bibliography (Section 1) provides an extensive record of this material, only significant additions since the second edition of *J. D. Salinger* by Warren French (1976) are listed here.

Davison, Richard Allan. "Salinger Criticism and 'The Laughing Man': A Case of Arrested Development." *Studies in Short Fiction* 7 (Winter 1981):1–15. A model for the reviews that are needed of the history of the criticism of each of the individual stories; however it is not quite successful because it shifts the center of attention from the children to the adults in the story.
Hipkiss, Robert A. *Jack Kerouac: Prophet of the New Romanticism,* pp. 97–105. Lawrence: Regents Press of Kansas, 1976. Salinger is discussed briefly, along with Ken Kesey and James Purdy, as another example of a new romanticism in American literature, principally exemplified by Kerouac.
Lewis, Roger. "Textual Variants in J. D. Salinger's *Nine Stories.*" *Resources for American Literature* 10 (Spring 1980):79–83. A start toward the textual study of Salinger's work, which is likely to be handicapped by the lack of manuscript materials available.
Lish, Gordon. "For Rupert—with Promise." *Esquire,* February 1977, 83–87. A difficult item to categorize, this parody of Salinger's work by the fiction editor of the men's magazine took on a critical dimension when readers accepted it as a pseudonymous example of Salinger's recent writing.
McSweeney, Kerry. "Salinger Revisited." *Critical Quarterly* 20, no. 1 (Spring 1978):61–68. Looking back over thirty years, McSweeney argues that *The Catcher in the Rye* is "the only work of Salinger's that has not shrunk with the passage of time," since Holden is "able to register," both the phoniness of the fallen world and the sense of wonder of the innocent world, though even it does not match Fitzgerald's mature accomplishment in *The Great Gatsby*.
Ohmann, Carol and Richard. "Reviewers, Critics, and *The Catcher in the Rye.*" *Critical Inquiry* 3 (Autumn 1976):15–37. The effort by two leading Marxist literary critics to determine how *The Catcher in the Rye* became a

classic, "a case study" of what capitalist critics saw in the novel and "what
they might have seen in it."

Pinsker, Sanford. *"The Catcher in the Rye* and All: Is the Age of the Formative
Book Over?" *Georgia Review* 40 (1986):953–67. Meditating that Salinger's novel encourages the "dreaming and heroic identification" that Lionel Trilling deplores, Pinsker reminisces about his seduction by Holden's
"authentic voice" and questions whether literature continues to exercise
such a formative influence.

Rosen, Gerald. "A Retrospective Look at *The Catcher in the Rye."* *American
Quarterly* 29 (Winter 1977):547–62. An attempt to look at Salinger's
novel as a "twentieth-century document" in the light of the enormous
amount of writing that has been done about it.

Stashower, Daniel M. "On First Looking into Chapman's Holden: Speculations on a Murder." *American Scholar* 52 (1983):373–77. A most provocative article on a specific question and the general problem beyond it,
which have received far too little attention from literary and sociological
critics. Mark David Chapman, who murdered John Lennon in December
1980, based his defense on what Strashower soundly observes is a misreading of *The Catcher in the Rye.*

Wiener, Gary A. "From Huck to Holden to Bromden: The Nonconformist
in *One Flew over the Cuckoo's Nest."* *Studies in the Humanities* 7, no. 2
(1979):21–25. Wiener follows up the extensive earlier analyses of Holden
Caulfield as continuing the rebel tradition of Huck Finn by tracing the
same pattern of behavior in Chief Bromden, who throws off institutional
restraints at the end of Ken Kesey's novel.

Yates, Richard. "Writers' Writers." *New York Times* 4 December 1977, sec. 7,
p. 3. In an appreciation that certainly deserves to serve as the last word
on Salinger, Yates cites him as "the living author he most admires," because "he used language as if it were pure energy beautifully controlled"
and "knew exactly what he was doing in every silence as well as in every
chord."

Addendum

Kurian, Elizabeth N. *A Religious Response to the Existential Dilemma in the Fiction
of J. D. Salinger.* New Delhi: Intellectual Publishing House, 1992. This first
scholarly treatise on Salinger from India is an erudite but engrossingly
readable account of how *"Zen* wisdom, *Christian* piety, *Hindu* philosophy
and *Jewish* fraternalism merge in his vision" to provide "an eclectic religious
perspective."

Index